GATE KEY

PRINTHOUSE BOOKS PRESENTS

Gate Key
Turning Your High School Education into Millions!
Business & Money

ANTWAN 'ANT' BANK$

ANTWAN BANK$

©2015 ANTWAN 'ANT' BANK$

Editor: Shelby Oates

Publication date: 3-1-2015

PrintHouse Books, Atlanta, GA.

www.PrintHouseBooks.com

VIP INK Publishing Group, Incorporated

All rights reserved. No parts of this book may be reproduced in any way, shape, form or by any means without permission in writing from the publisher or the author except by a reviewer.

GATE KEY

Cover art designed by SK7

ISBN: 978-0-9861-3403-6

Library of Congress Cataloging-in-Publication Data

ANTWAN "ANT" BANK$

Gate Key: *Turning Your High School Education Into Millions*/ ANTWAN "ANT" BANK$

1. Self Help 2. Business/Economics & Finance
3. Careers/Job Opportunities 4. Education/Teaching
5. ANTWAN 'ANT' BANK$

Printed in the United States of America

Gate Key: *Turning your High School Education Into Millions* attacks the glue that holds the very fabric of the higher learning institutions together. It gives hope to teens that find themselves in despair. It creates opportunity for those in lower class society who seem to be destined for a life of poverty and unemployment. It turns that one way street to becoming a criminal into an 8-lane highway of self-preservation. Gate Key will not only spark the flame to ignite the inner fire that we call a dream. It reveals over 30 lucrative professions that can be started while in high school or immediately after which will place our youth on a road to success without the need for a college education.

The awful truth is that only 4 out of every 7 teenagers will go on to attend college after graduating high school and for many reasons some will not complete this journey. Everyone wants the American dream for their kids; they want them to get a degree, find a great job, get married and have children, buy a house with a white picket fence then live happily ever after. Here's a shocker! The American dream will be just that for many of our youth, a dream! Too often teens can't afford college, have no interest in going, did not prepare for it, have kids early or are undecided any one of which causes them not to attend college and to head straight into the sub-par job market. Minimum wage can barely pay utility bills let alone take care of a family; this, more times than not, places our kids in the lowest class of society (in reference to a three-tier society of Lower Class, Middle Class or the Upper Class). This book gives our youth a choice as to what class they want to end up in, how much income they want to earn and how to begin that journey while still in high school without getting any student loans or attending any college. It will put our youth on track to become prosperous entrepreneurs and professionals by making them aware of career choices that they probably didn't even know existed for them as teens.

Gate Key doesn't only make our youth aware of these opportunities, but will show when, where and how to start one of these featured career paths while still a teen. This book is designed to open doors for those that cannot or will not be attending college after high school for some reason or another. Even now you have the power in you to be whoever you want to be! My purpose is to open your eyes to some of the many options that the world has to offer. After all, it was said best by our forefathers in **The Declaration of Independence**:

"We hold these truths to be self-evident, that all men are created equal, that they are endowed by their Creator with certain unalienable Rights, that among these are Life, Liberty and the pursuit of Happiness"

ANTWAN BANK$

My Story

I can remember the first day I decided to go after the American Dream. I had just graduated from Wilson High School in Florence S.C. and had been pondering my options the last few weeks before. I aspired to be an Architectural Engineer; it was a passion of mine as I aced my Junior and Senior High School years' vocational class of Mechanical Drawing so I was well on my way. High school was really like hanging out to me, I never really studied at all and my classes weren't really hard either. To be honest I went for the girls and to hang out with my boys. Then one day it just hit me! What the hell am I going to do for the rest of my life? Yeah, I said I wanted to be an Architect, but was that really what I wanted?

See, I was so busy not taking high school seriously that I didn't listen to the counselors my freshman and sophomore years when they tried to tell me what pre-college courses to take and how to choose a career. But, the sad part about that situation was that I was in the majority. None of us really even thought about our lives after high school until it was too late and life all of a sudden happened! It really starts at home and that's the God's honest truth. Too many of us are ignorant to the fact on how to prepare for adulthood.

I got my act together when I spoke with my uncle who was living in Columbia S.C. right behind

GATE KEY

Midlands Technical College. He himself was a scholar and prided himself on education. My Uncle Pete explained to me how to apply to college along with seeking financial aid. I was so excited after our talk that I left my mom's and sister's home in Florence two weeks after I graduated from high school to find a job in Columbia, S.C. close to the college. After applying accordingly, I got approved for The Pell Grant, selected a class schedule and was all set to start in August of 1989. Things were looking up and I was excited to be going to college. I even landed a job at the McDonald's on Garnersferry Road just a few blocks away from the apartment and the college campus.

The first day of class was not until August so I worked every hour that I could to save money to assist me with school during the prior months. The grant helped pay for my classes, but my job paid for my books and all the other things that I needed to continue my education. Weeks and weeks passed as I worked hard flipping burgers and depositing checks into my bank account to help fund my dream. The first day of school came and I enjoyed every minute. My days consisted of school, work, homework, a nap then school and work again. I didn't mind though because I saw the light at the end of the tunnel. A few months passed and I fell into my routine of school and work; life was so simple then.

I really believe that if you work hard at something it will pay off in the end. To this day I live by that! Work hard and stay consistent at it! Well, I remember doing just that one busy Saturday afternoon at McDonald's. It was one of those game day Saturdays when the Gamecocks hosted the Clemson Tigers, a big in-state rivalry. I was the only cook in the kitchen that day and all of the store managers were sitting in the front lobby with the regional manager having a meeting. I can still hear Tony, Tone, Toni's song playing over the restaurant speakers- "It feels good!"- on the Big DM radio station. As the music played, I kept the food coming, never falling behind for what seemed like two hours.

All of a sudden, the music stopped and all I could hear were fryers, toasters and ovens beeping as the grease popped off the beef patties. Then I heard someone yell my name. My shift manger Cynthia had called me to the side and asked if I was alright. I said, "Yeah, why you ask?"

She said, "Come with me!"

I followed her out to the lobby where the other managers sat with the owner and regional manager. They told me that I just handled the game day rush all by myself and that the line was backed up from the drive-through all the way to the street with cars even jammed in the turning lane waiting to get in the drive-through. I didn't think it was a big deal. I was only doing my job.

Because of my hard work, the owner and regional manager put me in The Manager's Program that same day. My two bosses, Donna and Lisa, whom I remember as two blonde-haired girls who should have been working at a mall or something, looked on in awe. My shift manager, Cynthia, took me straight to the office and gave me a manager's manual to take home and study. This was all cool, but I really didn't see it as a big deal until Cynthia told me that I would be making more money. That was music to my ears, more money for school! She said, "Study tonight, then when you come tomorrow I will have you start your training under me."

I left work excited that day, I even told all of my family and friends about the promotion. The next day at school was the norm, work, work, work! My plan was to get my Associate's at Midlands and then continue on to USC for another 4 years. I was focused; I had a nice balance of school and work combined with an ethic of hard work, so how could I fail? Life gives you challenges every day and sometimes it's the people that you least expect that will challenge you.

I remember walking to work elated about the new position and new salary. When I entered the restaurant, I didn't see Cynthia anywhere. Donna comes up to me as I'm clocking in and tells me that she wants me to clean the bathroom baseboards and the cracks between the wall tiles. I say, "Fine, no problem."

I clock in, put on my new manager trainee badge and get one of the workers to do it. As time goes by, Donna walks up to me then asks why I wasn't cleaning the baseboards like she asked. I told her that they were done. She replied, "But, I didn't see you leave the kitchen since you got here!"

I explained that I had told Tim to do it. Boy, why did I say that?! She turned cherry red and told me that I was supposed to do it! I told her, "I'm a manager trainee now and I shouldn't have to do it. My job is to make sure that it was done and it's done."

Well, Donna sent me home that day and told me to come back tomorrow and we were going to have a talk. I was furious because I depended on the money to pay for my books. I kept quiet though and left. I walked in the next day bothered from the day before, but didn't show it. Donna came up to me as I was clocking in again and asked me to clean the baseboards in the lobby with a tooth brush this time. I said, "Ok!"

She said, "No Antwan, you do it! Don't get someone else to."

I replied, "Excuse me?"

By now, I knew where this was going and this was the moment that changed my life forever. The tension had gotten thick between us while we were standing at that time clock. It seemed like those few seconds were really an hour as I contemplated my next move. Donna replied, "If you don't do it, you might as well clock out and don't come back." My life flashed before my eyes, all that I was working for had somehow come to this one stupid moment in time. To stay in school, I had to swallow my pride and go clean those damn baseboards!

I was so pissed. I didn't do anything wrong, nothing to deserve this! I went to school, studied, came to work and life was simple, hard, but simple. Now, because I'm a hard worker who got rewarded I have to deal with jealousy, racism or whatever the hell you want to call it?! I didn't care what it was, to me, it was wrong! So, I clocked out and told Donna to shove it!

ANTWAN BANK$

You should always keep a mental note in the back of your mind that your boss or employer will control your quality of life, if you don't. That includes the kind of car you drive, where you live, the clothes on your back and even the food in your fridge. Gate Key will inform you about some great career choices and give you some control over your own quality of life while restoring value to the high school education.

GATE KEY

I dedicate this book, my 13th release, to those of you who dare to dream and then turn your dream into a reality!

ANTWAN 'ANT' BANK$

Gate Key
Turning Your High School Education into Millions!
Business & Money

VIP INK Publishing Group, Incorporated.
Atlanta, GA.

GATE KEY

Gate Keys: *Attributes that you will need in order to be successful at making your dream a reality. There are 7 keys and each one is very important to your success.*

1. **Image**
2. **Character**
3. **Hard Work and Dedication**
4. **Qualifications and Certifications**
5. **Good Credit**
6. **No Criminal Record**
7. **Clean Driving Record**

(The Gate Keys will open doors to a great salary and quality of life.)

The Fraternity of Successful Dreamers

As you turn the page and begin reading through the names of the individuals who became successful with only a high school education, some college or very little schooling, if any, I ask that you forget about what you thought was the right way of doing things and consider the impossible to be very possible. Then think about which Gate Keys they used to open the doors to their dreams. Welcome to the journey that will now mold the rest of your life.

GATE KEY

Table of Contents

1.	Successful Dreamers	19
2.	Insurance Professional	156
3.	Firefighter	159
4.	Truck Driver	161
5.	Real Estate Agent	163
6.	Armed Forces	165
7.	Night Club Owner	168
8.	Auto Detail Shop	177
9.	Painter	181
10.	Landscaping	184
11.	Comedian	187
12.	Bail Bondsman	191
13.	Music Producer	194
14.	Custom Auto Painter	198
15.	Model	200
16.	Social Media Promoter	205
17.	Airline Pilot	209
18.	DJ	215
19.	Politician	219
20.	Film/Video Producer	225
21.	Online Business Owner	231
22.	Floor Installation Company	234
23.	Party Promoter	236
24.	Flight Attendant	240
25.	Photographer	242
26.	Chauffer Services	246
27.	Writer	249
28.	Staffing Agency	254
29.	Recording Artist	257
30.	Talent Agent	262
31.	Cleaning Services	266
32.	Dancer	269
33.	Sports Management Agency	271
34.	Business Entities	275

35. Licensing   281
36. Skill Sets   282
37. The 7 Gate Keys   284
38. Parent's Role   289

GATE KEY

William Adams, aka **Will.i.am**, singer, songwriter, music producer, founder of the Black Eyed Peas, actor, entrepreneur. He formed his first group in high school. Never attended college.

Ben Affleck, actor, screenwriter. Left the University of Vermont after one semester; then dropped out of Occidental College to pursue acting.

Andre Agassi, tennis player, winner of 8 Grand Slam titles. Quit school in the ninth grade and turned tennis pro at the age of 16. His father would drive the kids to school, but instead actually took them to local tennis courts to practice.

Christina Aguilera, singer, songwriter. Never finished high school.

Danny Aiello, actor. Dropped out of high school at the age of 16 to join the Army. Later received a high school equivalency degree.

Chuck Allen, banker, co-founder of the National Scholastic Surfing Association, and founder of the U.S. Amateur Snowboard Association. At the age of 19, he moved from Oklahoma to California and began working odd jobs until he was established enough to move on to a banking career.

Paul Allen, billionaire co-founder of Microsoft, founder of Xiant Software, owner of the Seattle Seahawks and Portland Trailblazers. Dropped out of the University of Washington to work for Honeywell. A year later he convinced Bill Gates to drop out of

Harvard and move to Albuquerque, New Mexico to start up Microsoft.

Woody Allen, screenwriter, actor, director, and producer. Was thrown out of New York University after one semester for poor grades. Also dropped out of City College of New York. As he admitted, "I was thrown out of college for cheating on the metaphysics final. I looked within the soul of the boy sitting next to me."

Joy Alukkas, billionaire jeweler. Never attended college. Immediately after high school, he moved to the Gulf to open a jewelry store.

Wally "Famous" Amos, multimillionaire cookie entrepreneur, author, talent agent. Dropped out of high school at the age of 17 to join the U.S. Air Force.

Paul Thomas Anderson, director of such movies as "Boogie Nights" and "Magnolia." He attended film school at New York University, but quit after two days because one professor dissed "Terminator 2" and another gave him a C for a writing assignment.

Tom Anderson, co-founder of MySpace. A high school dropout.

Mario Andretti, race-car driver, author. High school dropout who later earned an equivalency degree.

Anthony Andrews, actor. High school dropout.

Julie Andrews, Oscar-winning actress, singer, author. Dropped out of high school.

Jennifer Aniston, actress. Never attended college.

"Jennifer Aniston says getting a nose job was the best thing she ever did. But keep in mind, she didn't go to college, her marriage failed, her mom hates her, and she was in that Kevin Costner movie." — Danielle Fishel, *The Dish*

Carmelo Anthony, basketball player. Left college after his freshman year to play in the NBA.

Christina Applegate, actress. High school dropout.

Micky Arison, billionaire chairman of Carnival Cruise Line. Dropped out of the University of Miami.

Billie Joe Armstrong, front man for Green Day punk rock band. High school dropout. As he noted, "I finally realized that high school didn't make any sense for me then. So I quit."

Louis Armstrong, jazz musician, singer. Dropped out of high school.

Peter Arnell, advertising executive. Never attended college. Talked his way into the advertising business after graduating from high school.

Eddy Arnold, country music singer and member of the Country Music Hall of Fame. He was 11 when his father died, so he turned to singing at church picnics and other venues to support his family. By the age of 17, he was singing in nearby honky-tonks and made his first radio appearance. He debuted at the Grand Ole Opry in 1943. Between 1945 and 1983, 145 of his songs made the country charts, with 28 of them at #1. He sold more than 85 million records.

Mathangi Arulpragasam, aka M.I.A., rapper. Did not attend college.

Julian Assange, Wikileaks founder, software programmer. Studied mathematics at the University of Melbourne, but dropped out because other students were doing research for the Pentagon's Defense Advanced Research Projects Agency.

John Jacob Astor, multimillionaire businessman. America's first multimillionaire. High school dropout.

"Stone Cold" Steve Austin, WWE champion wrestler, actor. Dropped out of the University of North Texas a few credits shy of a physical education degree. Took a job as a freight dockworker. Then enrolled in the Dallas Sportatorium Wrestling School.

Gene Autry, singing cowboy, actor, songwriter, producer, businessman, author, baseball team owner. High school dropout.

Dan Aykroyd, actor, comedian. Dropped out of Carleton University in Ottawa, Canada.

Kevin Bacon, actor, singer, songwriter. High school dropout. At the age of 17, he moved to New York City to pursue a career as an actor. As he noted in an interview in *Elle* Magazine, dating older women "was the closest thing I had to a college education. I will always be grateful."

Pearl Bailey, singer, actress. Dropped out of high school.

Josephine Baker, singer, actress, dancer. High school dropout.

Lucille Ball, actress, comedienne, producer. Co-founder of Desilu Studios. Bought out her husband's share to become the first woman to own and run a production studio. Dropped out of high school.

Tyra Banks, supermodel, actress, TV host, and TV producer. Was all set to attend Loyola Marymount University, but deferred college when she received an offer to be a model in Paris, France.

Antwan 'ANT' Bank$, publisher, best-selling author, motivational speaker, founder and CEO of VIP INK Publishing Group, Incorporated / PRINTHOUSE Books. Dropped out of Midlands Technical College in the first year to join the U.S Army and went on to pursue his dreams.

"Teaching our youth to be successful by inspiring them to chase their dreams and pushing them to become business owners motivates me to succeed!"

Brigitte Bardot, actress, model, author, animal rights activist. High school dropout.

Roseanne Barr, actress, comedienne, producer, director. High school dropout.

Fantasia Barrino, singer, actress, *American Idol* winner, reality TV star. Dropped out of high school, but finally earned her GED in 2010.

Drew Barrymore, actress, producer, and director. High school dropout. Never attended college.

John Bartlett, author and publisher, *Bartlett's Familiar Quotations*. Did not attend college, but ended up owning the University Bookstore at Harvard University.

Bill Bartman, billionaire businessman, author. High school dropout.

Count Basie, bandleader, pianist. Dropped out of high school.

Warren Beatty, Oscar-winning director, actor, producer, and screenwriter. Dropped out of Northwestern University after his freshman year to attend Stella Adler's Conservatory of Acting. Beatty is one of the few people ever to receive Oscar nominations in the Best Picture, Actor, Directing and Writing categories from a single film (he did it twice for *Heaven Can Wait* and *Reds*).

Glenn Beck, radio and TV political commentator, best-selling book author. Enrolled at Yale University for one class, but quickly dropped out because he "spent more time trying to find a parking space" than in class.

Keep in mind, I am not anti-college. There is simply such a thing as getting an education other than through the gates of a university that are charging our children $100,000 to $150,000 to $250,000 just to be able to have a certificate that doesn't necessarily mean anything to them. I'm not anti-education. I am anti-massive debt. I am anti-giving our children's souls over to these universities.

Anne Beiler, multimillionaire, co-founder of Auntie Anne's Pretzels restaurants. High school dropout.

André Benjamin, aka André 3000, rapper, singer, songwriter, actor, member of OutKast. Dropped out of high school, but later earned a high school equivalency degree.

Tony Bennett, aka Anthony Benedetto, singer, artist. Attended New York City's High School of Industrial Art but dropped out at the age of 16 to support his family.

Jack Benny, actor, comedian, violinist. Dropped out of high school.

Irving Berlin, Oscar-winning songwriter, composer. When his father died when he was 8 years old, he had to work to survive. Wrote such long-lasting hits as *God Bless America, White Christmas, There's No Business Like Show Business*, etc.

Carl Bernstein, Watergate reporter, *Washington Post*. Never finished college. Started as a copy boy at the *Washington Star* at the age of 16.

Yogi Berra, baseball player, coach, and manager. Quit school in the eighth grade.

Chuck Berry, rock singer. High school dropout, left in the 11th grade. Received high school equivalency degree at the age of 37. Attended cosmetology school for a while when younger.

Halle Berry, Oscar-winning actress. After high school, she moved to Chicago to pursue a career in modeling. Did not attend college.

Patrizio Bertelli, billionaire co-founder of Prada fashion house. Dropped of engineering school to produce leather belts and handbags.

Jessica Biel, actress. Attended Tufts University for about a year and a half.

In an interview in *Glamour* Magazine, she said that leaving college was one the toughest choices she ever made: "I do still have a desire, a pang in my heart, when I think about it and the fact that I didn't spend my four years with my friends."

Manoj Bhargava, billionaire founder of 5-Hour Energy. Dropped out of Princeton University and returned to India to spend 12 years as a monk. Later developed the formula that made him rich.

Joey Bishop, actor, comedian. Never finished high school.

William Bishop, actor. Enrolled at West Virginia University, but got involved in Summer Theater and left college to tour with a *Tobacco Road* theater production. Later went to Hollywood and signed an MGM contract.

William Blake, poet, artist. Never attended school, educated at home by his mother.

Bobby "Blue" Bland, blues singer. Dropped out of high school and moved to Memphis, Tennessee, to sing in a gospel group.

Barbara Jean Blank, aka Kelly Kelly, model, wrestler, wrestling diva. Dropped out of college to become a wrestling diva.

Mary J. Blige, Grammy-winning singer, songwriter, record producer, and actress. Dropped out of high school in the eleventh grade.

Timothy Blixseth, billionaire founder of Yellowstone Club. Skipped college, failed as a professional songwriter. Made his first fortune as a timberland investor. At the age of 15, he bought 3 donkeys for $75 and resold them a week later as pack mules.

Orlando Bloom, actor. Left high school at the age of 16 to study acting. Later won a scholarship to the British American Dramatic Academy.

Humphrey Bogart, Oscar-winning actor. Flunked out of prep school at Andover.

Michael Bolton, Grammy-winning singer, songwriter. High school dropout.

Sonny Bono, singer, actor, songwriter, U.S. congressman. Dropped out of high school.

David Bowie, singer, songwriter, actor, record producer. Sold 136 million records. May not have graduated from high school. Did not attend college.

Ray Bradbury, award-winning science fiction author. Never went to college because his parents couldn't afford to send him. So, he sold newspapers on Los Angeles street corners during the day and educated himself at libraries at night. "I never went to college. I went to the library." He graduated from the library at the age of 28.

Marlon Brando Jr., Oscar-winning actor. Expelled from Libertyville High School for riding his motorcycle through the school. Later attended Shattuck Military Academy, but was also expelled from there. Was invited to come back, but he decided not to finish school.

Buck Brannaman, horse whisperer, rancher. At the age of 17 he began working with the great horseman Ray Hunt. Did not attend college. He was the inspiration for Robert Redford's movie *The Horse Whisperer.*

GATE KEY

Richard Branson, billionaire founder of Virgin Music, Virgin Atlantic Airways, Virgin Mobile, and other Virgin enterprises, balloonist. Left Stowe School when he was 16. Never attended college.

Ralph Braun, founder of BraunAbility, inventor of battery-powered scooters and wheelchair lifts. Attended college at Indiana State for a year, but dropped out.

Jacques Brel, Belgium singer, songwriter, actor, and director. Did not finish high school. Never attended college.

Jeff Bridges, Oscar-winning actor, singer. Joined the Coast Guard Reserve rather than attending college.

Sergey Brin, billionaire co-founder of Google. Dropped out of Stanford Ph.D. program in computer science to start Google in 1998 working out of a friend's garage. He eventually finished the Ph.D. program, so at this point he's no longer a college dropout.

Christie Brinkley, aka Christie Lee Hudson, model, actress, political activist. After graduating from high school in Los Angeles, she moved to the Left Bank of Paris, France.

Pierce Brosnan, actor. He left school in England at the age of 15 to draw and paint. He also did odd jobs like washing dishes, cleaning houses and driving a cab. But, as he noted, "Once I found the world of theater, I was off to the races!"

James Joseph Brown, mining engineer, husband of Unsinkable Molly Brown. Self-educated.

Margaret "Molly" Brown, socialite, philanthropist, social activist, survivor of the Titanic. High school dropout.

Joy Bryant, model, singer, surfer, snowboarder. Dropped out of Yale University to become a Victoria's Secret model and, later, the face of CoverGirl.

Bebe Buell, singer. Did not go to college. Went to New York to become a model, but became a singer and rock star paramour (and mother of actress Liv Tyler).

Warren Buffett, billionaire chairman of Berkshire Hathaway. Dropped out of the University of Pennsylvania after two years. But, later he did get his bachelor's degree and MBA.

Stuart Burguiere, radio talk show host, producer. He slacked his way through high school and did not attend college. Here's what he has to say about college:

"We're damning our children to hundreds of thousands of dollars in debt. Before they work a day in their life - and they spend over half the time there in recreation. It's insanity."

Gisele Caroline Bündchen, Brazilian multimillionaire supermodel. High school dropout. Left home at the age of 14 to begin her modeling career. Moved to

New York City at the age of 16 to continue her career as a model. "Reading things is so important to me — things that can open up your mind. You need to feed your mind."

Solomon Burke, singer, the King of Rock and Roll, preacher, actor, entrepreneur. Never attended college.

Ronald Burkle, billionaire supermarket owner and investor, Yucaipa. Dropped out of California State Polytechnic University and returned home to work in a Stater Brothers grocery store. Had started early stocking shelves; joined union local as a box boy at age 13.

Mark Burnett, TV producer, *Survivor* and other reality shows. Joined the British Army at the age of 17. Never attended college.

George Burns, Oscar-winning actor, comedian. Elementary school dropout.

Robert Byrd, U.S. senator. Graduated from high school, but could not afford to attend college.

James Francis Byrnes, U.S. representative, U.S. senator, Supreme Court justice, U.S. secretary of state, South Carolina governor. At the age of 14, he left St. Patrick's Catholic school to apprentice in a law office. Never attended college or law school.

James Cagney, actor, song-and-dance man. Worked from the age of 14 as an office boy, janitor, package wrapper, and finally vaudeville dancer.

Hector "Macho" Camacho, boxer. Expelled from six schools by the age of 16. Turned professional boxer at the age of 18. Did not attend college.

James Cameron, Oscar-winning director, producer, and screenwriter. Dropped out of California State University, Fullerton, at the age of 20. Then took up street racing while working as a truck driver and a high school janitor, eventually getting a job building models for Roger Corman's New World Pictures.

Naomi Campbell, model, TV host. She was discovered by a modeling scout at the age of 15. Did not attend college.

Vince Camuto, founder of Nine West footwear and the Camuto Group. Never attended college. After high school, he became a service manager at a shoe store.

Lizzy Caplan, actress. Was accepted at New York University, but decided not to attend so she could continue to act. As an actress in the *Mean Girls* movie, she got a taste of the college experience: "It was interesting because that movie was as close to a college experience as I got."

George Carlin, comedian, author, four-time Grammy winner. Never finished high school. As he noted, "The fact that I didn't finish school left me with a lifelong need to prove that I'm smart." He also noted, "When you're a dropout and the culture accepts you and begins to quote you and teach your stuff in class and textbooks, this is my honorary baccalaureate."

GATE KEY

Kitty Carlisle, actress, panelist on *To Tell the Truth*. "I went to boarding schools in Lausanne. And then I went to school in Neuilly. I stopped school when I was about 16. I went to Rome to come out. I never got any degrees or anything, but I am better educated than people who went to college."

John Carmack, founder of Armadillo Aerospace, cofounder of Id Software (sold 10 million copies of Dome and Quake games). At the age of 14, he was sent to a juvenile home after breaking into a school to steal an Apple II computer. Quit college early to become a game programmer.

Andrew Carnegie, industrialist and philanthropist. Elementary school dropout. Started work at the age of 13 as a bobbin boy in a textile mill. One of the first mega-billionaires in the U.S.

Adam Carolla, comedian, radio/TV personality, podcast superstar. "He was a wrong-side-of-the-tracks North Hollywood high-school graduate who could barely read and who worked a series of menial jobs before breaking into radio and then TV" (*Fast Company*). Did not attend college.

Scott Carpenter, astronaut. He twice flunked out of the University of Colorado.

Jim Carrey, actor, comedian. Dropped out of high school.

Julia Carson, U.S. congress representative, did not graduate from college. She was the first woman and first African American to represent Indianapolis.

Amon G. Carter, multimillionaire oilman, civic promoter, newspaper publisher, *Fort Worth Star-Telegram*. Never finished eighth grade.

Gary Carter, Hall of Fame baseball player. He was heavily recruited to play college football, but chose to sign with the Montreal Expo baseball team instead.

Tom Carvel, inventor of the soft-serve ice cream machine, founder of Carvel ice cream stores. Did not attend college. Before he began selling ice cream, he was an auto mechanic, Dixieland band drummer, and test driver for Studebaker.

John Catsimatidis, billionaire oilman and real estate magnate, founder of the Red Apple supermarkets. Studied engineering at New York University, but dropped out to help a friend save his family's supermarket business. Owned 10 stores of his own by the age of 24 with $25 million per year in income. During college, he "did not study much. Would not tell my kids that."

Bruce Catton, historian, editor of *American Heritage*, author. World War I interrupted his studies at Oberlin College. He tried twice after the war to finish college but kept getting pulled away by real jobs at a succession of newspapers.

GATE KEY

Jackie Chan, actor and philanthropist. A grade school dropout. He attended the China Drama Academy, became an accomplished student of martial arts and acrobatics, and began work in films at the age of 8.

Subhash Chandra, billionaire founder of Zee TV satellite television channel. Dropped out of college to help his family. Became a rice trader and later founded Essel Propack.

Coco Chanel (Gabrielle Bonheur Chanel) fashion designer. Left the orphanage at the age of 18 to pursue a career as a cabaret singer.

Do Won Chang, billionaire founder of Forever 21 retail chain. Never attended college.

Jin Sook Chang, billionaire founder of Forever 21 retail chain. Never attended college.

Charles Chaplin, Oscar-winning actor, screenwriter, producer, director. Dropped out of elementary school.

Ray Charles, singer, pianist. Dropped out of high school.

Dov Charney, founder of American Apparel. Started the company when he was a high school senior. Never attended college.

Binod Chaudhary, Nepal's first billionaire, hotel owner, banker, and more. Skipped college to join his family trade at the age of 18.

Winston Churchill, British prime minister, historian, artist. Rebellious by nature, he generally did poorly in school. Flunked sixth grade. After he left Harrow, he applied to the Royal Military Academy at Sandhurst, but it took him three times before he passed the entrance exam. He graduated 8th out of a class of 150 a year and a half later. He never attended college.

Madonna Ciccone, multimillionaire pop singer and actress. Dropped out of the University of Michigan, where she was studying dance, to move to New York to pursue a singing career.

Kelly Clarkson, pop singer. Got several college music scholarships, but passed on them to move to Los Angeles to pursue a singing career.

Grover Cleveland, U.S. president (22nd and 24th). Dropped out of school to help his family. Studied law while clerking at a law firm. Of the 43 people who served as president of the United States, 8 never went to college.

Eleanor Clift, reporter, *Newsweek*. No college degree. Went to night school for several years while working as a secretary.

Hank Cochran, country singer and songwriter. Worked in the oil fields of New Mexico while still a teenager. Then moved to California to sing before moving to Nashville and building a career as a songwriter of such hits as "I Fall to Pieces," "Make the World Go Away," and "She's Got You." Never graduated from high school.

GATE KEY

Paulo Coelho, songwriter, bestselling novelist. Was institutionalized from age 17 to 20. He later enrolled in law school, but dropped out after one year, became a hippie, traveled the world, and later worked as a songwriter before writing his first novel. His novel *The Alchemist* has sold more than 100 million copies.

Jackie Collins, actress and novelist. Expelled from high school at the age of 15. She immediately threw her school uniform into the Thames River and never looked back. She has written 28 bestselling novels so far with 400 million copies sold worldwide.

Phil Collins, actor, singer, songwriter, drummer, keyboardist. Never attended college. Solo singer as well as lead singer for Genesis.

John Collison, software wizard, co-founder of Stripe. Dropped out of Harvard to start Stripe, the online service for accepting payments on the web.

Patrick Collison, software wizard, co-founder of Stripe. Dropped out of MIT during his freshman year to help two friends develop and eventually sell Automatic for millions of dollars.

Christopher Columbus, explorer, discover of America. Little formal education. Home schooled.

Christine Comaford-Lynch, founder of Artemis Ventures (venture capital firm) and Mighty Ventures. Dropped out of high school. Later also dropped out of the University of California at San Diego and UCLA.

Dabbled as a model, trained as a geisha, spent years as a Buddhist monk, dated Bill Gates and Larry Ellison. She is the author of *Rules of Renegades*.

Sean John Combs, rapper, producer, fashion designer, entertainer, actor, and entrepreneur. Did not finish college. As he said in an interview in *Time* Magazine, "I'm just not that type of person. As soon as I got out of the womb, I was ready to do this. Then there's other times—I'm not really high-tech computer savvy, and there's some things that I do have weaknesses with. I don't know if school would have made that better for me. I'm cool the way I've turned out."

Sean Connery, Oscar-winning actor. Dropped out of high school.

Harry Connick, Jr., Grammy-winning pianist, singer, actor. Has sold over 25 million albums. At the age of 18, he left New Orleans to move to New York City. Did study at Loyola University, Hunter College, and the Manhattan School of Music, but apparently did not graduate.

Kevin Connolly, actor. Skipped college, moved to Los Angeles to live with a bunch of unemployed actors and finally had success as an actor in *Entourage*.

Casey Connor, celebrity DJ. When her mother and father died when she was 16, she started an in-home day care center so she could keep her 12-year-old sister out of foster care. She is now a celebrity DJ in great demand in the LA area. While she never attended college, she is most proud of helping her sister get through college.

Lauren Conrad, reality show actress, bestselling novelist, fashion designer. Moved to Los Angeles fresh out of high school to pursue acting. Never attended college.

Jack Kent Cooke, billionaire media mogul, owner of Washington Redskins football team. Dropped out of high school.

James Fenimore Cooper, novelist. Was kicked out of college for a prank.

Al Copeland, multimillionaire founder of Popeye's Fast Food. Left high school at the age of 16 to work in a supermarket and later at a doughnut shop. While he never finished high school, he supported educational programs through his donations.

Rick Corman, founder of R J Corman Railroad Group. Founded the company in 1973 when he was 18 years old. Did not attend college.

Don Cornelius, creator, producer, and host of *Soul Train* TV show; the high priest of soul, funk, and disco. Joined the marines after high school, then sold insurance, finally became a radio DJ on a local AM radio station before founding *Soul Train* with $400 of his own money.

Steve Corona, chief technology officer of Twitpic. Dropped out of the Rochester Institute of Technology in his sophomore year.

I basically said, going to class is not worth my time. I ended up failing out. I was 19 or 20 years old, making 10 bucks an hour at a little job, and I was like "Holy crap, I'm screwed." ...

You need to have a history of making things, a history of being successful outside college. You need that inner fire when exploring things outside what you're doing in the classroom. I didn't really give myself that diagnostic test, but looking back, I see that I was doing things on my own, I was building stuff outside of the classroom. I was building all sorts of web applications. I was doing web hosting online, and I remember the thrill of running my own company. The first time a dollar came in, even though it was only a dollar, it was such a thrilling roller coaster, I just wanted more of it.

Source: http://www.fastcompany.com/3005641/innovation-agents/portrait-dropout-twitpic-cto-steve-corona

Simon Cowell, TV producer, music judge, *American Idol, Britain's Got Talent,* and *The X Factor*. A member of Forbes 2008 Celebrity 100, he made $72 million in 2007. He dropped out of boarding school at the age of 16.

Courteney Cox, actress, model, producer. Moved to New York City at the age of 18 to pursue acting and modeling. Did not attend college.

GATE KEY

James M. Cox, newspaper publisher, 3-term governor of Ohio, presidential nominee in 1920, founded Cox Enterprises. A high school dropout.

Simon Crane, stunt person and stunt coordinator for movies. Dropped out of law school and joined the circus before starting stunt work in a James Bond movie.

Cindy Crawford, actress, model, entrepreneur. Graduated high school as the valedictorian. Then studied chemical engineering at Northwestern University for half a year before dropping out to model.

Joan Crawford, Oscar-winning actress, dancer. Dropped out of high school.

Davy Crockett, frontiersman, U.S. congressman. Less than six months of formal education. Home schooled.

Tom Cruise, actor, producer. Never attended college.

Roy Cullen, oilman billionaire. Dropped out of fifth grade.

Charles Culpeper, multimillionaire owner and CEO of Coca Cola. Dropped out of high school.

Brunello Cucinelli, billionaire fashion designer. Dropped out of engineering school. "In three years I completed one exam."

Elisha Cuthbert, actress. Took off for Los Angeles right after high school to develop her acting career. She gave herself six months to succeed. During the last week of those six months, she got a key role in the 24 TV series. Has not yet attended college.

Miley Cyrus, singer, actress. Has not yet attended college.

Nic Dahlquist, Android developer at Snapchat. Took a leave of absence from Stanford University to work at Snapchat.

John Daly, professional golfer. Dropped out of the University of Arkansas to launch his career as a professional golfer.

Claire Danes, actress. Attended Yale University where she did all the rebellious things - getting drunk and partying - that she'd missed out on as a teenager. She left after two years to return to acting, but did say that "College was just so essential for my sense of self and my development."

Sharon Daniels, author, *The World of Truth*. "Eventually I came to conclude that I could not find real knowledge in academic life, only hierarchies of knowledge that led, ultimately, to more hierarchies, not to more knowledge. I began to see university learning as limited, human, and relative. What was seen as absolutely up-to-date did not consider the infinite and timeless."

Jim Danielson, founder of Makt Systems. Dropped out of Purdue University for at least two years to work on developing an electric motor that can be retrofitted into any car. Funded $100,000 by Peter Thiel, co-founder of Paypal, via his college dropout project.

Sammy Davis, Jr., singer, actor, comedian. Never finished high school.

Rosario Dawson, actress and political activist. Did not graduate from college, but she did take pre-calculus and calculus at the Cooper Union and a civil-engineering course at Columbia. She is a firm believer in the value of education.

Dorothy Day, journalist, socialist, political activist, pacifist, anarchist, suffragist. Co-founder of the Catholic Worker movement. Attended the University of Illinois at Urbana-Champaign on a scholarship, but dropped out after two years to move to New York City to become a social activist.

James Dean, actor. Attended Santa Monica College, but transferred to UCLA where he dropped out during his sophomore year to pursue a career as an actor.

Jimmy Dean, singer, songwriter, actor, multimillionaire founder of Jimmy Dean Foods. Dropped out in the 9th grade to join the Merchant Marines at the age of 16. Later joined the Air Force at the age of 18. After getting out of the Air Force, he and his band, the Texas Wildcats, developed a following in Washington state.

Darwin Deason, billionaire entrepreneur, founder of ACS. Left his hometown the day after graduating from high school for Tulsa, Oklahoma, where he got into data processing. Later took over MTech, which he sold in 1988.

Paula Deen, restaurant owner, TV chef, bestselling cookbook author. Did not attend college. After high school, she married at the age of 18 and soon learned how to cook great meals.

Ellen DeGeneres, comedienne, actress, talk show host. Dropped out of the University of New Orleans. As she noted in an interview with Us Magazine, "I didn't go to no college."

John Paul DeJoria, billionaire co-founder of John Paul Mitchell Systems hair care products and founder of Patron Spirits Tequila, Gustin Energy, DeJoria Diamonds, and other companies. Joined the U.S. Navy right out of high school. After the Navy, he spent time doing many odd jobs, sometimes living out of a car, before finding work selling hair care products.

I learned sales and marketing from knocking on a hundred doors a day. You quickly discover that you'll get 99 slammed in your face before you make a sale. (quoted in The Education of Millionaires by Michael Ellsberg)

GATE KEY

Michael Dell, billionaire founder of Dell Computers, among top ten wealthiest Americans. Founded his company out of his college dorm room. Dropped out of the University of Texas at the age of 19 to run the company.

Dom DeLuise, comedian, actor. Graduated from high school, but never attended college. Instead, he began acting at the Cleveland Play House.

Leonardo Del Vecchio, founder of Luxottica. Did not attend college. Began as an apprentice to a tool and dye maker of molds for auto parts and eyeglass frames. Started Luxottica at the age of 23. Now world's largest maker of sunglasses and prescription eyewear.

Patrick Demarchelier, fashion photographer. His stepfather gave him a Kodak camera when he was 17. He started working at a photography store right away and never attended college.

Patrick Dempsey, actor, "Dr. McDreamy", juggler, race car driver. Dropped out of high school in Lewiston, Maine to travel as a juggler, unicyclist, and singer. He went on to a stage-acting career and finally stardom on TV.

Robert De Niro, Oscar-winning actor, producer. Dropped out of high school.

Felix Dennis, multimillionaire magazine publisher, *Maxim*, *Blender*, and others. Left home before his sixteenth birthday and dropped out of art college.

I got rich without the benefit of a college education or a penny of capital but making many errors along the way. I went from being a pauper, a hippie dropout on the dole, living in a crummy room without the proverbial pot to piss in, without even the money to pay the rent, without a clue as to what to do next... to being rich. — Felix Dennis, magazine publisher, *How to Get Rich*

Johnny Depp, actor. Never finished high school.

Richard DeVos, billionaire co-founder of Amway (now Alticor), owner of the Orlando Magic basketball team. Served in the Army after high school. Founded Amway along with his best friend Jay Van Andel.

Cameron Diaz, model and actress. Moved from modeling in her teens to acting in her 20s. Did not attend college.

Maria Diaz, CEO and founder of Pursuit of Excellence. Dropped out of college as a recent widow to work three jobs and care for her son. Later worked for Jenny Craig. Then set up a coaching practice that led to founding Pursuit of Excellence.

Leonardo DiCaprio, actor. At the age of 14, he signed with an agent and began doing commercial work as well as acting. He completed high school with a tutor, but put off college. As he has noted, "Life is my college now."

Charles Dickens, bestselling novelist. Left elementary school to work in a factory after his father was thrown into debtors' prison. Although he had little formal education, his early poverty drove him to succeed.

Bo Diddley (Ellas Otha Bates), rock & roll singer, songwriter, and guitarist. Never attended college.

Barry Diller, billionaire, Hollywood mogul, Internet maven, chairman of IAC/InterActive Corp (owner of Ask.com, Ticketmaster, CitySearch, Evite, LendingTree.com, etc.). The son of a wealthy real estate developer, he attended Beverly Hills High School, but dropped out of UCLA after four months to work in the mail room of William Morris.

Joe DiMaggio, baseball player, husband of Marilyn Monroe. High school dropout.

Walt Disney, producer, director, screenwriter, animator, developer of Disneyland. Winner of 26 Oscars and 7 Emmy awards. While attending McKinley High School, he also took night classes at the Chicago Art Institute. He dropped out of high school at the age of 16 to join the Army. Rejected because he was under aged, he joined the Red Cross and was sent to war in Europe. Upon his return from war, he began his artistic career.

Snoop Dogg, rapper and actor. Never attended college. "A lot of people like to fool you and say that you're not smart if you never went to college, but common sense rules over everything."

Laurann Dohner, erotic romance novelist. Has made the *New York Times* and *USA Today* bestseller lists. Dropped out of high school during the 11th grade. Has not attended college.

Charles Dolan, billionaire founder of HBO which he traded to Time, Inc. for Cablevison cable provider. Also owns Madison Square Garden, the New York Knicks, and the New York Rangers. Dropped out of college.

Thomas Dolby, musician, composer, music producer. Dropped out of high school.

Jack Dorsey, billionaire founding CEO of Twitter, co-founder and CEO of Square. Dropped out of New York University and bounced between jobs before landing at Odeo, the forerunner of Twitter.

Robert Downey, Jr., actor. Dropped out of Santa Monica High School during his sophomore year (another source says his junior year).

Drake, rapper, actor. Dropped out of high school when he landed a role in the Canadian TV series, *Degrassi: The Next Generation*. Graduated from high school at the age of 26. As he noted, it was "one of the greatest feelings in my entire life."

Francis Drake, British admiral and explorer. Home schooled.

Michael Clarke Duncan, actor. Dropped out of Alcorn State University when his mother became ill.

Worked as a ditch digger and bouncer to support her. He later moved to Los Angeles and became a bodyguard before finding success as an actor.

Dominique Dunne, actress. Went to the University of Colorado to study acting, leaving after one year to pursue her career as an actress.

Tom Dwan, millionaire online poker player. Dropped out of Boston University. He started with a $50 investment and built it into millions playing poker online.

Bob Dylan, singer and songwriter. Dropped out of the University of Minnesota and moved to New York City to seek out his idol Woody Guthrie. Has honorary degrees from Princeton University and St. Andrews (Scotland).

Johnny Earle, founder of Johnny Cupcakes. Dropped out of music school to sell limited-edition T-shirts out of the trunk of his '89 Camry. The *Boston Globe* has named him one of the most innovative business leaders in Massachusetts.

George Eastman, multimillionaire inventor and founder of Kodak. High school dropout.

Clint Eastwood, Oscar-winning actor, director, and producer. Attended at least half a dozen schools and excelled at none of them. Enrolled at Los Angeles City College, but never graduated. Among other jobs, he bagged groceries, delivered papers, fought forest fires, and dug swimming pools. Also worked as a steelworker and logger.

Mark Ecko, founder of urban-wear company Mark Ecko Enterprises. Left Rutgers University during his third year to start his company with his sister, Marci, who also left college to work on the business.

Thomas Edison, multimillionaire inventor of the phonograph, light bulb, and many other inventions. He quit formal schooling after his teacher called him addled. Was home-schooled by his mother. Joined the railroad at the age of 12.

John Edson, billionaire leisure craft manufacturer. Dropped out of the University of Washington. Started building boats in his garage.

Zac Efron, actor, singer. Had been accepted by the University of Southern California, but chose to continue pursuing acting instead. He hasn't ruled out more study. His biggest regret? Not going to college.

Daniel Ek, cofounder of Spotify, software engineer. After high school, he enrolled at the Royal Institute of Technology in Sweden to study engineering. After eight weeks, he dropped out. Via programming he became a millionaire by the age of 23.

Duke Ellington, bandleader, composer. Dropped out of high school.

Larry Ellison, billionaire co-founder of Oracle software company. Dropped out of the University of

Chicago after one year. Later also dropped out of the University of Illinois. Then discovered computer programming.

Queen Elizabeth II, Queen of England. Tutored at the palace. Did not attend school.

Eminem, rapper. Has a limited formal education, but "by the time I was 18 I had probably read the dictionary front to back like 10 times."

Jennifer Esposito, actress, model, dancer. Has not attended college. After discovering she has celiac disease, she founded Jennifer's Way (http://www.jennifersway.com) to help others to learn how to live gluten-free. Has written a cookbook and founded a gluten-free bakery.

Eric Ethans, cofounder of Suja Juice, dropped out after two years at Golden West College to open a raw food restaurant.

Shawn Fanning, developer of Napster. Dropped out of Northeastern University when 19 to move to Silicon Valley to further develop Napster. He made the cover of *Time* and *Fortune* at the age of 19, months before he dropped out of school!

Perry Farrell (Peretz Bernstein), musician, Jane's Addiction, Porno for Pyros, and Satellite Party. Also, producer and founder of the Lollapalooza music tour. Never attended college.

William Faulkner, Nobel and Pulitzer Prize-winning novelist. Dropped out of high school after his second year. Also later attended, but dropped out of the University of Mississippi.

David Feherty, golfer and TV show host. Dropped out of school at the age of 17 to play golf.

Arash Ferdowsi, millionaire cofounder of DropBox.com. Dropped out of MIT to start up DropBox.com.

Fergie, aka Stacy Ann Ferguson, singer, songwriter, fashion designer, actress. A straight 'A' student and cheerleader in high school. Went on a Rock-and-Roll spree after turning 18, while touring with Wild Orchid. Never attended college.

Craig Ferguson, late night talk show host. As he noted recently, "Economists are saying that a college degree may not be necessary to succeed in life. Look at me, I didn't go to college and here I am. Seriously kids, go to college."

Patrick Leigh Fermor, travel writer. Expelled from King's School in Canterbury, he left school at the age of 18 to walk across Europe (which he then wrote about in two books).

Enzo Ferrari, founder of the Scuderia Ferrari Grand Prix motor racing team and later the Ferrari car manufacturer. Grew up with little formal education.

GATE KEY

Mel Ferrer, actor, director, producer, husband of Audrey Hepburn. Dropped out of Princeton to get into acting.

Tilman Fertitta, billionaire owner of Landry's Restaurants and Golden Nugget Casinos. Dropped out of Texas Tech University and the University of Houston.

Sally Field, Oscar-winning and Emmy-winning actress. Never attended college.

Debbi Fields, founder of Mrs. Fields Cookies. Founded the company when she was a 21-year-old mother with no business experience. Did not graduate from college.

Laurent Fignon, professional bicyclist, two-time winner of the Tour de France. Left the University of Villetaneuse to join the Army. Did not complete college.

Millard Fillmore, U.S. president. Six months of formal schooling. Studied law while a legal clerk for a judge and law firm. Of the 44 people who served as president of the United States, 8 never went to college.

David Filo, billionaire co-founder of Yahoo! Dropped out of Stanford University PhD program to create Yahoo!

Carly Fiorina, CEO, Hewlett-Packard. Disappointed her parents by dropping out of law school after one semester.

Paul Fireman, multimillionaire owner of Reebok. Dropped out of Boston University to take over his family's sporting-goods business.

Bobby Fischer, Grandmaster chess player. A high school dropout.

Ella Fitzgerald, singer. Dropped out of high school.

F. Scott Fitzgerald, novelist. Dropped out of Princeton University.

Bobby Flay, TV chef, restaurateur, and cookbook author. Bored with high school in New York, he dropped out at the age of 17 to work as a line cook at the Joe Allen Restaurant. Allen was so impressed with Flay's talent that he paid to send him to the newly opened French Culinary Institute. Two years later, Flay graduated from the institute and began his career as a chef.

Sean Flynn, actor, photojournalist. Son of Errol Flynn, Sean left Duke University after his freshman year to star in *The Son of Captain Blood*. He later became a famous photojournalist covering the Vietnam War where he apparently died (MIA and still unaccounted for).

Charles Foley, inventor of the Twister party game and 96 other inventions. Dropped out of school after the eighth grade and served in the Michigan Air National Guard before getting a job in a design studio.

Danielle Fong, cofounder of Lightsail Energy. One day, when she was a junior in high school in Nova Scotia, she realized that the "doors were unlocked and I could just walk away." She did. After dropping out from junior high school, she enrolled in a local college. By the age of 17, she enrolled in a PhD program at Princeton University. Again she dropped out to become an entrepreneur.

I noticed that my professors, who were brilliant people, were spending most of their time applying for grants. I thought it would be more efficient to make my fortune first and then invest it in energy research. - from an interview in *Forbes* magazine

Harrison Ford, actor. Dropped out of Ripon College. He worked as a carpenter for almost ten years before finding success as an actor in *Star Wars* and other movies.

Henry Ford, billionaire founder of Ford Motor Company. Received only a modest rural education. Left his home on the farm to work as an apprentice machinist for James Flower & Brothers in Detroit, Michigan. Later ran a sawmill and became a chief engineer for Edison Illuminating Company before starting the Ford Motor Company.

George Foreman, heavyweight champion boxer, author, designer of the George Foreman Lean Mean

Fat-Reducing Grilling Machine. Quit school in the ninth grade, but did get his GED. Never attended college.

Megan Fox, actress. Tested out of high school via correspondence and moved to Los Angeles. Landed a role in a movie after only two months. Never attended college.

Michael J. Fox, actor. Dropped out of high school. Got his GED when he was in his 30s. Co-starred in a Canadian television series at the age of 15. Left Canada at the age of 18 to go to Hollywood to pursue an acting career.

Jeff Foxworthy, comedian, author, and actor. Dropped out of Georgia Tech.

Dick Francis, novelist, jockey. Dropped out of school at the age of 15 because his father, as noted by the *London Times*, felt "that a day's hunting or show jumping was more valuable" than formal schooling.

Justin Frankel, multimillionaire software programmer, developer of WinAmp and Gnutella, founder of Cockos, Inc. Attended the University of Utah for two quarters, but then dropped out. A few months later, he released the first version of WinAmp, a free MP3 player.

Aretha Franklin, singer. Dropped out of high school.

Benjamin Franklin, inventor, scientist, diplomat, author, printer, publisher, politician, patriot, signer of the U.S. Declaration of Independence. Dropped out of Boston Latin. Home schooled with less than two years of formal education.

Joe Frazier, heavyweight boxing champion. Never finished high school. Left home at the age of 15 to go to New York City.

Markus Frind, software programmer, multimillionaire founder of Plenty of Fish dating website. Graduated from technical school with a two-year degree in computer programming. Did not attend any further higher education.

Robert Frost, poet. Dropped out of Dartmouth College.

Eden Full, founder of Roseicollis Technologies. Dropped out of Princeton University for at least two years to work on her solar panel design. Funded $100,000 by Peter Thiel, co-founder of Paypal, via his college dropout project.

R. Buckminster Fuller, inventor of the geodesic dome, visionary, philosopher, poet, architect, futurist. He never finished college, after being expelled from Harvard twice (one involving some chorus girls).

J. B. Fuqua, industrialist, philanthropist. Never attended college, but learned about business by checking out books from the Duke University library through the mail. Later donated $36 million to support a business school at Duke.

Clark Gable, Oscar-winning actor. High school dropout.

Lady Gaga, aka Stefani Joanne Angelina Germanotta, rock singer and songwriter. Dropped out of NYU at the age of 19 to pursue her music career full time.

Amancio Ortega Gaona, billionaire fashion entrepreneur, third richest man in the world (early 2013). Born in poverty, he could not afford to go to college. He dropped out of high school and got a job at a local clothing store. He went on to found and build the Zara retail empire.

Bill Gates, billionaire co-founder of Microsoft, one of the richest men in the world, philanthropist. Dropped out of Harvard after his second year to work with Paul Allen on the venture that became Microsoft. As he noted, "I realized the error of my ways and decided I could make do with a high school diploma."

Richard Gere, Golden Globe-winning actor. Dropped out of the University of Massachusetts at Amherst after two years.

David Geffen, billionaire founder of Asylum Records and Geffen Records and co-founder of DreamWorks. A dyslexic, he dropped out of the University of Texas at Austin after his freshman year. He also flunked out of Brooklyn College. Admittedly, he has said, "I was a lousy student." He started his career in entertainment by sorting mail at the William Morris Agency. He got that job by faking a degree from UCLA.

GATE KEY

Alan Gerry, billionaire cable TV executive, philanthropist. He dropped out of high school during World War II to join the Marines. He then trained as a TV repairman on the GI bill. In 1956, he launched his cable business with $1,500.

George Gershwin, songwriter, composer. High school dropout.

J. Paul Getty, billionaire oilman, once the richest man in the world. Failed to graduate from the University of Southern California, Berkley or Oxford University.

Amadeo Peter Giannini, multimillionaire founder of Bank of America. High school dropout.

William Gibson, science fiction novelist, first to use the word cyberspace. He was orphaned at the age of 18. To avoid the draft and the war in Vietnam, he moved to Canada where he worked odd jobs. Years later he finally finished his first novel, *Neuromancer*. He never attended college.

Daniel Gilbert, psychology professor at Harvard University. Dropped out of high school, but later earned an equivalency diploma.

Dizzy Gillespie, musician, songwriter. Dropped out of high school but later received an honorary diploma from the high school he attended.

Jackie Gleason, actor and comedian. With 36 cents in his pocket, he left home after his mom died while he was still in his teens. He soon moved beyond amateur night shows and began working as a professional. He never finished high school.

John Glenn, astronaut, U.S. senator. Did not finish at Muskingum College in Ohio. According to Wikipedia, "In April 1959, despite the fact that Glenn failed to earn the required college degree, he was assigned to the National Aeronautics and Space Administration (NASA) as one of the original group of Mercury astronauts."

Sam Goi, billionaire owner of Tee Yih Jia Food Manufacturing, the Popiah King. Dropped out of school to work in his father's grocery store.

Whoopi Goldberg, Oscar-winning actress, comedienne, talk show host. Dropped out of high school, worked as a bricklayer and trained as a beautician before hitting it big as a comedienne.

Hyman Golden, multimillionaire cofounder of Snapple. A high school dropout and one-time window washer.

Barry Goldwater, U.S. senator and presidential candidate. He dropped out of the University of Arizona after one year to take over the family department store.

Bob Goodson, CEO, YouNoodle.com. Dropped out of Oxford University where he was studying for a master's degree in medieval literature and philosophy.

GATE KEY

Steffi Graf, tennis star. Turned professional in her teens when she ran out of players good enough to challenge her. Never attended college.

Laurence Graff, billionaire jeweler. At the age of 15, he was apprenticed to a London jeweler. Did not attend college.

Kelsey Grammar, actor. Attended Juilliard for two years, but was kicked out for poor attendance. Went on to acting success in *Cheers*, *Frasier*, and *Back to You* television shows.

Jacques-Antoine Granjon, multi-millionaire founder of Vente-Privee flash sale site. Failed his entrance exam to the Sciences Polytechniques in France. Started his career buying non-selling fashion clothing and selling it via discount outlets.

Cary Grant, Oscar-winning actor. High school dropout. Left home at the age of 16 to become an acrobat and later an actor.

W.T. Grant, multimillionaire founder of W.T. Grant Department Store chain. High school dropout.

Pat Gray, radio talk show host. He originally got a job in radio as a teenager in order to save money for college, but when it was time to go to college, he realized he was already doing something he loved and was making a living at it. So he stayed with it.

Horace Greeley, newspaper editor and publisher, U.S. congressman, presidential candidate, co-founder of the Republican Party. Dropped out of high school.

David Green, billionaire founder of Hobby Lobby, religious philanthropist. Did not attend college. Started the Hobby Lobby chain with a $600 loan.

Mart Green, multimillionaire founder of Mardel Retail Stores, CEO of Bearing Fruit Communications (aka EthnoGraphic Media), CEO and executive producer for Every Tribe Entertainment, chairman of the board of Oral Roberts University. Dropped out of college after one year. Founded Mardel at the age of 19.

Philip Green, billionaire retail mogul, Topshop. Dropped out of high school to apprentice with a shoe importer.

Skylar Grey, singer, songwriter. Moved to Los Angeles at the age of 17 with a record deal, but went broke. So she worked her way up the coast doing odd jobs until she came up with her first hit song. Has not yet attended college.

Ken Grossman, multimillionaire co-founder of Sierra Nevada. Dropped out of Cal State Chico to manage a bike shop and then opened a home brewing supply store.

Bob Guccione, Penthouse publisher. Did not attend college.

GATE KEY

Gene Hackman, actor. Discharged after six years in the Marines, he entered college as a journalism major, but after six months he dropped out for good. Since then he's earned an Academy Award for best actor (*The Conversation*) and an Academy Award for best supporting actor (*Unforgiven*).

Aviv Hadar, CEO of Think Brilliant web-development studio and the tech brains behind SoulPancake. Dropped out of college.

Thomas Haffa, billionaire German media mogul. Dropped out of high school.

Larry Hagman, actor and director. Attended Bard College for one year, but then dropped out to begin acting at Margo Jone's theater in Dallas, Texas. Went on to star in the *Dallas* soap opera (twice now).

Jerry Hall, supermodel. A few weeks before her 17th birthday, she flew to Paris to pursue a modeling career. She later married rock stars Bryan Ferry and Mick Jagger. Never attended college.

Joyce C. Hall, founder of Hallmark. Started selling greeting cards at the age of 18 while living at a YMCA in Kansas City. Did not attend college.

Josh Halloway, actor. Did not attend college.

Keith Gordan Ham, aka Swami Bhaktipada. Became an American leader in the Krishna movement before being expelled for "moral and theological deviations."

Dropped out of graduate studies at Columbia University to become a disciple of Hare Krishna.

Dorothy Hamill, Olympic ice skater. Did not attend college.

Harold Hamm, billionaire oil wildcatter, Continental Resources, Hiland Holdings. Left home at the age of 17, married, but finished high school a year later. Became a gas jockey before becoming a wildcatter. He later took college classes in geology, chemistry, and mineralogy, but never graduated from college.

Armie Hammer, actor. He was kicked out of one high school for burning its name on the grass outside the school. He did not graduate from college: "I tried college at UCLA. I gave it a fighting effort and I just couldn't do it." Another time he noted: "I didn't care about college. I knew I wanted to make movies."

Chelsea Handler, TV host, producer, comedienne, bestselling author. Dropped out of community college and moved to Los Angeles at the age of 19 to pursue a career as an actress. She waited tables for the first six years until she got a spot on the *Girls Behaving Badly* prank show.

Taylor Handley, actor. Began acting as a teenager. Moved to Los Angeles after high school graduation to pursue acting full-time. Has not yet attended college.

Tom Hanks, Oscar-winning actor. Dropped out of CalState University after a few years to work as an intern at the Great Lakes Theater Festival.

GATE KEY

William Hanna, cartoonist, Hanna-Barbera. He briefly attended college, but dropped out at the beginning of the Great Depression.

Matt Harding, game designer, world traveler, YouTube dancing viral star. Never attended college. As he notes in his bio (http://www.wherethehellismatt.com/about): *Matt was a mediocre student and never went to college. When he got older, he was pleased to discover that no one cares.*

Mariska Hargitay, actress. After being crowned Miss Beverly Hills at the age of 18, she started getting small acting jobs, but didn't really break through until her 30s. Attended UCLA, but left before graduating to pursue her acting career. *(Law & Order, SVU)*

Angie Harmon, actress and model. After graduating from high school, she headed to Europe to work as a model. She has never attended college.

Martha Matilda Harper, business entrepreneur, founder of the Harper Hair Salons. At the age of seven, she was sent to work as a domestic servant. Worked as a servant for 22 years before saving enough money to start a hair salon. Never attended college.

Ciara Princess Harris, crunk & B singer, songwriter, and actress. Signed with LaFace Records at the age of 16. Has not yet attended college.

Lorenz Hart, lyricist. At the age of 21, he had everything he needed from Columbia University academics, so he left college without a degree and began translating song lyrics.

Lucy Hart, actress. When she was 15, she moved with her mother from Tennessee to Los Angeles to pursue a career as an actress. Has not yet attended college.

Melissa Joan Hart, actress, singer, director, producer, candy store operator. Started acting at the age of 3. Appeared in hundreds of commercials before getting the job of acting in the *Sabrina* TV show. Attended New York University for two years, but deferred further studies when she got the TV show.

Sheldon Harvey, Navajo artist, winner of the Best of Show at the 2008 Santa Fe Indian Market. Dropped out of high school to care for his wife and son. "When I dropped out of school, no one in my family thought it was the end of the world. My grandparents were from the old school, traditional people who didn't think an education was necessary to make your way in the world." He later convinced the people at Dine Community College to let him attend even though he had not graduated from high school. He took classes there, but apparently did not graduate.

Anne Hathaway, actress, *The Princess Diaries*. Began acting professionally at the age of 16. Briefly attended Vassar and New York University, but has not graduated from either.

Rutger Hauer, actor. Dropped out of school to join the Dutch merchant navy. After his discharge, he went to acting school before starting a career as an actor. Did not attend college.

Leif Hauge, inventor. Never finished college.

Louise Hay, one of the bestselling authors in history and founder of Hay House. Of other famous women authors, *Levine Breaking News* has noted, "They did not change the spiritual landscape of America and several of its Western allies. They were not pregnant at 15 and they did not lack high-school diplomas." Louise Hay did.

Amber Heard, actress. Got her GED and quit a Catholic high school during her junior year to move to New York to be a model. Finding modeling unrewarding, she moved to Hollywood to become an actress. At 17, she landed a small role in the movie *Friday Night Lights*. Has not attended college.

William Randolph Hearst, newspaper publisher and movie producer, was thrown out of Harvard for poor grades (apparently due to heavy partying).

Richard Heckmann, billionaire investor, CEO of U.S. Filter, founder of Heckmann Corporation. Went to college in Hawaii, but did not graduate. "I went to Vietnam in '65 and was assigned to the 33rd Air Rescue Squadron. When I came back in '66, I wasn't in any mood to go back to school. I got a job selling insurance." He later attended the Harvard Business School small-company management program.

Levon Helm, rock singer, member of The Band. Left home at the age of 17 to play music. Never attended college.

Sherman Hemsley, actor. Dropped out of high school and served in the Air Force for four years before returning home to work in a post office while trying out for acting jobs in his spare time. Eventually found success as George Jefferson in *All in the Family* and *The Jeffersons* TV shows.

Christina Hendricks, model and actress. At the age of 18, she moved to New York to become a model. Has not yet attended college.

Diane Hendricks, billionaire co-founder of ABC Supply, the largest supplier of roofing and siding materials to contractors. Never attended college.

Kenneth Hendricks, billionaire co-founder of ABC Supply, the largest supplier of roofing and siding materials to contractors. Dropped out of high school, never attended college, and eventually joined the family roofing company.

Kevin Hendricks, roofing store operator. Skipped college to go into the roofing business. His high school graduation present was $100, a nail bag, and a roofing hammer. Later, he turned a money-losing store into ABC Supply's biggest profit center.

Jimi Hendrix, rock 'n roll guitarist. A high school dropout.

Patrick Henry, Virginia governor, revolutionary patriot. Home schooled. Later studied on his own and became a lawyer.

John Henton, actor, comedian. Never finished at Ohio State University. "I never ended up going back to Ohio State. I just wanted to be a comedian, you know, and I was getting a good response."

John Hewitt, CEO of Jackson Hewitt. College dropout.

Stanley Ho, billionaire casino operator, King of Gambling. Dropped out of college.

Lillian Hochberg, founder of Lillian Vernon catalog. Did not attend college. Started the catalog out of her home.

Amanda Hocking, multi-millionaire self-publisher, novelist, blogger. A few months of college.

I went to college, but I only went to my writing class, so I dropped out after a semester. A few years later, I went to college again, but I only went to my English class, so I dropped out after a semester.

Eric Hoffer, longshoreman, philosopher, and author. A self-educated philosopher, he was at various times a dishwasher, lumberjack, gold prospector, migrant farm worker, and longshoreman. He is the author of *The True Believer, Working and Thinking at the Waterfront,* and *Reflections on the Human Condition.*

Dustin Hoffman, two-time Oscar-winning actor. Enrolled at Santa Monica College, caught the acting bug after taking an acting class for an easy grade, then left after a year to join the Pasadena Playhouse.

Elizabeth Holmes, billionaire founder and CEO of Theranos. Left Stanford University's School of Engineering to build Theranos around her patents and vision for healthcare.

Ernest Holmes, founder of the Science of Mind churches and author of *The Science of Mind*, ended his formal schooling when he was fifteen.

Katie Holmes, actress. Her acceptance letter for Columbia University came a week after she did the pilot for the *Dawson's Creek* TV show. She spent the next six years acting in the TV series. She now admits that going to college as a celebrity would be very difficult. "But," she says, "maybe I could hire a cute professor to home-school me."

Odetta Holmes, the queen of American folk music, singer, songwriter, actress, and human rights activist. Studied music at night at the Los Angeles City College, but did not graduate.

Dennis Hopper, actor. Did not attend college, but did study acting at the Old Globe Theater in San Diego and the Actors' Studio in New York City. When people asked him what school he went to, he would reply "Warner Bros."

GATE KEY

Jay Catherwood Hormel, multimillionaire president of Hormel Foods, inventor of Spam. Left college to work for his father's company.

Whitney Houston, Grammy-winning singer and actress. At the age of 19, she was discovered singing in a New York City supper club by Clive Davis, who immediately signed her to a contract with Arista Records. Her first album, and the next six, all went multi-platinum. She is in the *Guinness Book of World Records* for being the most awarded female artist of all time. Her soundtrack for *The Bodyguard* is the bestselling soundtrack album of all time.

Hugh Howey, millionaire novelist, self-publisher, and bookseller. Dropped out of college. Was working in a bookstore when he began writing and publishing a series of sci-fi novellas called *Wool*.

John Hughes, director, producer, and screenwriter. Dropped out of Arizona State University in his junior year.

D. L. Hughley, sales manager, actor, comedian. Never finished high school. He got his job as a sales manager by paying "a guy I knew at Cal State Long Beach $100 to tell personnel that I was just a few credits short of graduating from college."

H. Wayne Huizenga, billionaire founder of WMX garbage company, builder of Blockbuster Video chain, owner of the Miami Dolphins. Skipped college to join the Army. Later dropped out of Calvin College after three semesters. Started business in 1962 with a used garbage truck.

Haroldson Lafayette Hunt, billionaire oilman. Only had a fifth grade education. Worked as a farmhand until he invested $50 in an Arkansas oil field.

John Huston, Oscar-winning director, actor. High school dropout.

Gary Hustwit, author and publisher, Incommunicado Press. Dropped out of San Diego State.

John Hutchison, discoverer of the Hutchison Effect. Had no formal schooling after the 8th grade although he was privately tutored in radio astronomy, chemistry, and physics.

Lauren Hutton, first supermodel, actress. Attended Sophie Newcomb College in New Orleans while working at a bar. Met Steve McQueen and got into acting. Dropped out of college.

Don Imus, national radio host, bestselling book author. Dropped out of college after a week.

Julie Inouye, actress, singer, health care advocate. Dropped out of Chico State University after dancer Harold Lang told her that she should be in New York or Los Angeles (after he had heard her sing).

Kathy Ireland, model, actress, CEO of Kathy Ireland Worldwide, book author. She admits that she barely graduated from high school. Did not attend college.

GATE KEY

Now runs a multi-million dollar licensing and product creation business.

Gregory Isaacs, reggae singer. Did not attend college.

Burl Ives, Oscar-winning actor, folk music singer. Dropped out of Eastern Illinois State Teachers College (now Eastern Illinois University) during his junior year. As he was sitting in an English class listening to a lecture on *Beowolf*, he realized he was wasting his time and walked out of the class and out of college.

Andrew Jackson, U.S. president, general, attorney, judge, congressman. Orphaned at 14. Home schooled. By the age of 35 without formal education, he became a practicing attorney. Of the 44 people who served as president of the United States, 8 never went to college.

Curtis "50 Cent" Jackson III, rapper, entrepreneur, producer, actor, book author, amateur boxer. Dropped out of high school in the 10th grade. Began dealing drugs at the age of 12. Began rapping professionally at the age of 21.

As he later noted, "If I had a choice, I would've been a college kid. I would've majored in business."

Reggie Jackson, baseball player. Attended Arizona State University for two years before he was drafted by the Kansas City Athletics.

Jane Jacobs, author, political activist, urban planner. After high school, she worked at a variety of office jobs and as a freelance writer. She studied for two years at Columbia University's extension school, but did not graduate.

Brian Jacques, author of the *Redwall* children's book series, never attended college. At the age of 15, he signed up to be a merchant seaman and then went on to work as a truck driver, boxer, longshoreman, folk singer, and bobby. He was in his 40s when he wrote his first story. His *Redwall* books have sold more than 20 million copies worldwide.

Micky Jagtiani, billionaire retailer, Landmark International. After flunking several exams he dropped out of accounting school in London. He then started out cleaning hotel rooms and driving a taxi. Eventually he started a retail business in the Middle East.

T. D. Jakes, pastor, bestselling novelist. Dropped out of high school.

Betty Mattas James, CEO, James Industry. Named the Slinky toy. Member of the Toy Industry Hall of Fame. She attended Pennsylvania State University, but left when she married Richard James, who later invented the Slinky. More than 300 million Slinkies have been sold.

Etta James, singer, queen of R&B. Signed as a recording artist when she was still a teenager. Never attended college.

GATE KEY

Josh James, multimillionaire co-founder of Omniture. Dropped out of Brigham Young University during his final semester to co-found MyComputer.com, which became Omniture.

Kevin James, aka Kevin George Knipfing, comedian and actor. Attended the State University of New York at Cortland, but dropped out of college after his junior year (after taking a course in public speaking) to perform stand-up comedy.

P. D. James, mystery novelist. Her greatest regret is "that I didn't go to university."

Thomas Jane, actor. He dropped out of football at Thomas Wootton High School in Rockville, Maryland to pursue acting. He eventually received his high school degree, but never attended college.

Jim Jannard, billionaire founder of Oakley and inventor of the Red One digital camera. He dropped out of USC School of Pharmacy to found Oakley.

Alex Jeffreys, Internet marketing millionaire. Never attended college. Hated school.

Brandon Jennings, basketball player. He was the first high school player to skip college and jump straight into pro basketball in Europe.

Claudia Jennings, model and actress. At the age of 10, she enrolled at Marquette University to study dramatic arts. Dropped out to pursue a career as a model and actress. Known as the Queen of the Drive-

In for such classics as *Gator Bait* and *Truck Stop Women*, she also starred in a number of mainstream movies and TV shows. She died in an auto accident at the age of 29.

Peter Jennings, news anchor, ABC's *World News Tonight*. Failed the 10th grade. Left high school at 16 to work as a bank teller. He later attributed his failure in high school to boredom and laziness.

Chris Jericho, aka Chris Irvine, WWE world champion wrestler, actor, author, radio and TV host, rock musician. Never attended college.

Derek Jeter, baseball player, set a New York Yankee record as their all-time hit leader. Chose to become a professional baseball player rather than attend college.

Steve Jobs, billionaire co-founder of Apple Computers and Pixar Animation; Disney's largest shareholder. Dropped out of Reed College after six months and went to India before returning to Silicon Valley. As he said, "I had no idea what I wanted to do with my life and how college was going to help me figure it out."

Billy Joel, singer and songwriter. A high school dropout.

John Johannesson, founder of Bauger Group fashion retailing group, finished Commercial College in Iceland (the equivalent of something between high school and junior college in the U.S.) and then launched a discount grocery with his father.

Jon Lech Johansen, software programmer, developer of DoubleTwist. At the age of 15, he wrote a program to decrypt commercial DVDs. He dropped out of high school to continue working on additional anti-DRM software programs.

Andrew Johnson, U.S. president, vice-president. Never attended college. Of the 44 people who served as president of the United States, 8 never went to college.

Bruce Johnson, cosmetologist and owner of Avatar Salon & Wellness Spa. Dropped out of the University of Maryland 26 credits shy of an engineering degree to study cosmetology. "I wasn't loving engineering. I was just doing it. ... I don't think I would have been as stimulated by a career in engineering. I wanted to be happy and successful," he says. "You're not supposed to leave college. It was a struggle. But, my heart was in this." Now his clients include former Secretary of State, Condoleezza Rice.

Kenny Johnson, founder of Dial-A-Waiter restaurant delivery service. Dropped out of Wichita State University.

Samuel Jonas, chief operating officer, IDT. Dropped out of Rutgers and Ramapo College.

Alan Jones, founder of Check Into Cash, former CEO of Credit Bureau Services. Dropped out of Tennessee State University to work at his father's credit agency.

Alex Jones, radio show host, documentary movie producer, founder of InfoWars.com and PrisonPlanet.tv. Briefly attended Austin Community College in Austin, Texas, but dropped out early. Has been criticized for not having a degree.

January Jones, model, actress. Left home three days after graduating from high school to go to New York to become a model. Later became an actress.

Jeremy Jones, snow boarder, film star. Did not attend college. Moved to Jackson Hole, Wyoming to pursue his passion as a snowboarder.

John Paul Jones, patriot, Navy admiral. Home-schooled. Went to sea early.

Quincy Jones, musician, composer, music producer, music executive, and more. Attended the Berklee College of Music, but left when he got the opportunity to tour with Lionel Hampton's band as a trumpeter, arranger and pianist.

Molly Jong-Fast, novelist. Went to Barnard, Wesleyan, and New York University for a semester each. Never finished college.

Louis C.K., actor, comedian, writer, director, producer. Did not attend college.

I thought about going to NYU film school--that was this ideal to me. But, I didn't make any kind of grades in high school. My mother was a single mom, putting my three sisters through college, and I was such a bad student that I knew I had no right to take her money. But, I loved classes and learning.

Henry J. Kaiser, multimillionaire founder of Kaiser Aluminum. High school dropout. He was apprenticed as a photographer's apprentice when he was 13. At the age of 20 he bought the business.

Travis Kalanick, billionaire founder and CEO of Uber ride-sharing service. He dropped out of UCLA.

Rob Kalin, multimillionaire founder of Esty (a website that helps artisans sell handmade crafts and clothing). He flunked out of high school, briefly enrolled in an art school, and then faked an MIT student ID so he could take classes on the sly. His professors were so impressed that they helped him get into NYU where he learned how to build a website. He founded Esty with two classmates.

Jeffrey Kalmikoff, cofounder and chief creative officer of Treadless.com. He never graduated from college.

Dean Kamen, multimillionaire inventor of the Segway. He dropped out of Worcester Polytechnic Institute.

Ingvar Kamprad, billionaire founder of IKEA, one of the richest people in the world. A dyslexic, he never attended college. When he was 17, his father gave him a reward for succeeding in his studies. He used this money to establish what became IKEA. As a child, he peddled matches, Christmas decorations, fish, and other sundries via his bicycle.

David Karp, founder of Tumblr. At the age of 11 he taught himself how to write code. He dropped out of Bronx Science at the age of 15 to be home-schooled and work for his Davidville Company. Did not attend college. At the age of 17, he moved to Japan and worked remotely for an American internet company. Founded Tumblr at the age of 20.

Donna Karan, fashion designer. Dropped out of Parsons School of Design at the age of 18.

Alex Karras, football player, actor. Never graduated from college. As he pointed out, "I never graduated college, but I was only there for two terms - Truman's and Eisenhower's."

Li Ka-Shing, billionaire, one of the wealthiest investors in Asia, plastics manufacturer, real estate investor. Had to leave school at the age of 12 to work in a plastics factory in order to support his family after his father's death.

Byron Katie, spiritual leader and author. Dropped out of the University of Northern Arizona before the end of freshman year to get married.

Ben Kaufman, serial entrepreneur, founder of Kluster (a virtual forum that allows consumers and businesses to collaborate on the design of products and services). Dropped out of college in his freshman year.

Elaine Kaufman, owner of Elaine's restaurant, a Manhattan cultural institution. She barely passed high school. Did not attend college.

George S. Kaufman, playwright and critic. After graduating from high school, he tried law school for three months, grew disenchanted, and went on to various odd jobs. Eventually he became a drama critic and later a playwright.

Diane Keaton, aka Diane Hall, actress. Flew to New York City at the age of 19 to try finding success as an actress. Attended acting schools, but never completed any college.

Michael Keaton (Michael John Douglas) actor. Dropped out of Kent State University after two years.

Bil Keene, cartoonist. His parents couldn't afford to send him to art school after high school, so he worked as a newspaper messenger at the *Philadelphia Bulletin* before joining the Army during World War II (where he drew a comic strip for *Stars & Stripes*). After the war, he became a staff artist at the *Bulletin*.

Toby Keith, country music singer. After high school, he joined his father to work in the oil fields. His biggest regret, though, is never having attended college.

Brad Kelley, billionaire landowner and founder of Commonwealth Brands Cigarettes. Never attended college.

Minka Kelly, actress, nurse. Attended one year of nursing school and became a surgeon's assistant. Went on casting calls in her free time. Finally got an acting job on the *Friday Night Lights* TV show.

Anna Kendrick, actress. Postponed college in 2004 to act and has not yet attended college. Became active as an actress at the age of 12 (acting in a Broadway show).

Kirk Kerkorian, billionaire investor and casino operator, owner of MGM Movie Studio, Mirage Resorts, and Mandalay Bay Resorts. He dropped out of eighth grade to pursue amateur boxing. He later trained fighter pilots during World War II. After the war, he founded Trans World Airlines.

Alicia Keys, singer and songwriter. Graduated from New York's Professional Performing Arts School at age 16. She enrolled at Columbia University, but dropped out after a semester to sign with Columbia Records.

Jewel Kilcher, singer and songwriter. Scored a major recording contract at the age of 18. At the time she had been traveling around California singing at coffee houses and sleeping in her car. Her first album sold 11 million copies. Has not attended college.

GATE KEY

Jared Kim, founder of WeGame. Dropped out of the University of California at Berkeley halfway through the spring semester of his freshman year to devote himself full-time to starting the online gaming site WeGame.

B.B. King, blues musician, songwriter, and legend. Never finished high school. "I have two laptops. I didn't finish high school, so one is my tutor: I buy software on things I don't know. I write music with the other." (*People* Magazine)

Pat Kingsley, publicist to the stars, president of PMK. Dropped out of Winthrop College after two years, eventually becoming a publicist.

Eartha Kitt, Emmy-winning actress, dancer, singer, author, and sex kitten. She dropped out of the High School of Performing Arts to take various odd jobs. Eventually landed a job with the Katherine Dunham dance troupe.

I am learning all the time. The tombstone will be my diploma. - Eartha Kitt

Karlie Kloss, model, fashion designer. Has not yet attended college.

Chris Klein, actor. Completed only two semesters at TCU before starring in the *American Pie* movies.

Heidi Klum, German supermodel, actress, fashion designer, television producer, and host of *Project Runway* and *Germany's Next Top Model*. One of Forbe's

2008 Celebrity 100, she makes $14 million per year. Became a model immediately after graduating from high school.

"I think that risk-taking is intelligent. When you do things you normally don't do, you learn about yourself – you change, and you evolve. Change is important." – Heidi Klum, model

Mike Koenigs, millionaire Internet entrepreneur and co-founder of Traffic Geyser. Never attended college.

Allan Kornblum, author, poet, and publisher, Coffee House Press. Dropped out of New York University.

Bruce Kovner, billionaire hedge fund operator, founder of Caxton Associates, chairman of Julliard. Dropped out of a Ph.D. economics program at Harvard to drive a taxi in New York City.

Jan Kramer, ice skater, actress, country singer. "The day I graduated from high school, I left for New York City," where she began acting in *All My Children*. Soon after, she left for Los Angeles to pursue her acting career, get parts on *90210*, *Entourage*, and *Friday Night Lights* before getting a role on *One Tree Hill*.

David Kravitz, early employee at Snapchat. Dropped out of Stanford to work on Snapchat.

Ray Kroc, multimillionaire founder of McDonald's. High school dropout.

Chad Kroeger, frontman for Nickelback rock group. In a *Playboy* magazine interview, he noted that "I didn't go to school. I mean, after the eighth or ninth grade, I don't remember going to school five days out of the week, ever." He was a few credits short of graduating from high school when he left school and took to the road.

Bernard Kroger, founder of Kroger supermarkets. Went to work at the age of 13 to help support his family. Never attended college.

Stanley Kubrick, movie director and producer, screenwriter, photographer. His poor high school grades made it impossible to attend college. He did take some photography classes at CCNY, but never graduated from any college.

Mila Kunis, actress. She briefly attended college, but had an epiphany: "I decided I wasn't going to take [my career] seriously and make my job who I am. I just want to be happy with my life."

During the production of *That '70s Show*, she had attempted to go to college, but soon realized that L.A. traffic made it virtually impossible to go to school at 6:00 a.m. and still make it to work at 10:00 a.m. She was the first person in her family not to become a college graduate.

Olga Kurylenko, model, actress, Bond girl. Began modeling at the age of 14 in Moscow, Russia. Soon moved to Paris, France for more modeling work. Then moved on into acting. Has not attended college.

Ashton Kutcher, actor, producer, entrepreneur. Dropped out of the University of Iowa to become a model.

Nick Lachey, singer and actor. "I was trying to be an athletic trainer. That's what I was studying in school when I quit to do music."

James Lafferty, actor. Has not yet attended college. But, he did note in an interview that if he weren't an actor, he'd "be a junior in college."

Don LaFontaine, voice-over artist who narrated more than 350,000 commercials, thousands of TV promos, and more than 5,000 movie trailers. After graduating from high school and serving in the Army, he went into business as a voice-over artist. He never attended college.

Peter La Haye, Sr., inventor of plastic replacement lenses for cataract patients, owner of La Haye Laboratories and Neoptx. Dropped out of high school.

Frederick "Freddy" Laker, billionaire airline entrepreneur. Dropped out of high school.

Miranda Lambert, country singer. Began singing as a professional while still in high school. Did not attend college.

Sharmen Lane, millionaire mortgage wholesaler, life coach, motivational speaker. A high-school dropout.

GATE KEY

Cathy Lanier, Chief of Police of Washington, DC. A 14-year-old pregnant high school dropout.

Angela Lansbury, Tony and Golden Globe award-winning actress. She was contracted by MGM while still a teenager and nominated for an Academy Award for her first film, *Gaslight*, in 1944. Her Broadway stage work earned her four Tony Awards in sixteen years for *Mame, Dear World, Gypsy,* and *Sweeney Todd*. But, she never won an Emmy for her work on the *Murder, She Wrote* television series. She also won six Golden Globes and was nominated for 18 Emmys and 3 Academy Awards. She never attended college.

Ring Lardner, sportswriter and short story writer. Began his career as a teenager writing for the *South Bend Tribune*. He continued writing for many other newspapers, eventually landing a nationally syndicated column for the *Chicago Tribune*.

Stan Lark, rock musician, Fireballs. Dropped out of New Mexico State University (actually dropped out days before classes were to begin) to become a rock star.

Albert Lasker, advertising pioneer, CEO of Lord & Thomas. After graduating from high school, he started at an advertising agency as an entry-level salesman.

Tommy Lasorda, baseball manager. Dropped out of high school.

Queen Latifah, aka Dana Elaine Owens. Singer, songwriter, rapper, actress, television producer, record producer, talk show hostess. Never attended college. Has won the following awards: Golden Globe, Grammy Award, Screen Actors Guild (and been nominated for many more).

Cyndi Lauper, singer, songwriter, actress. Left home at 17 to work a number of odd jobs and sing in bars until she was able to break through as a bestselling singer.

Jillian Lauren, author. Quit New York University during her freshman year to become a party guest for a wealthy Singapore businessman. Went on to live in the harem of the Prince of Brunei for a year-and-a-half. Wrote about her experiences.

Ralph Lauren, billionaire fashion designer, founder of Polo. Dropped out of the City College of New York business school (Baruch College) to design ties for Beau Brummel. Launched Polo later that same year.

Avril Lavigne, singer, songwriter, actress, fashion designer. Dropped out of high school.

Peter Lawford, actor. Never finished high school.

Annie Lawless, cofounder of Suja Juice, dropped out of law school to become a yoga instructor.

Jennifer Lawrence, actress. She started acting at the age of 14 and has been in demand since then. Has not yet attended college.

Mike Lazaridis, billionaire founder of Research in Motion. "Two months before I graduated from college, I answered a request for proposal from General Motors with a five-page pitch to develop a network computer control display system. They offered me a half-million dollar contract.... I went to the president of the university to get his permission to take a leave of absence. He tried to persuade me to finish out my year, but when I told him about the contract, he wished me the best of luck." Since that time, he hasn't had time to go back and finish.

David Lean, Oscar-winning director. Dropped out of high school.

Harper Lee, Pulitzer Prize-winning author, *To Kill a Mockingbird*. Dropped out of college during her senior year. Moved to New York to become a writer.

Sandra Lee, TV show host, entrepreneur, cookbook author, magazine editor. Spent three years at the University of Wisconsin at La Crosse before founding a craft company.

Stan Lee, comics creator, Marvel Comics (*Spiderman, The Hulk, X-Men, The Fantastic Four*). Started working when he was still in high school. Never attended college.

Anna-Lou "Annie" Leibovitz, portrait photographer, cover photographer for *Vanity Fair* and *Rolling Stone* magazines. Attended the San Francisco Art Institute, but apparently did not graduate. As she has said, "I was very lucky, in working for these magazines, to learn by doing, but I always regretted not having a formal education. I had to teach myself."

Tim Leiweke, CEO of Anschutz Entertainment Group. Skipped college to get into sports management.

Tia Leoni, actress. Dropped out of Sarah Lawrence College as a 20-year-old to model and act.

James Leprino, billionaire, Leprino Foods. Joined family business at the age of 18. Turned business into the world's largest mozzarella producer.

Doris Lessing, novelist. At the age of 14, she chose to end her formal schooling. She then worked as a nanny, telephone operator, office worker, stenographer, and journalist. Her first novel was published when she was 31. She won the Nobel Prize for Literature in 2007.

Aaron Levie, multi-millionaire software developer, co-founder of Box.net. Dropped out of the University of Southern California in 2005 to create Box.net.

Aaron Levine, fashion designer, vice president of Club Monaco. Left Virginia Tech to work at Abercrombie & Fitch. Never finished college.

Jerry Lewis, comedian, actor, singer, humanitarian. High school dropout.

Joe Lewis, billionaire businessman. Dropped out of high school.

Juliette Lewis, actress, singer, musician. At the age of 14, she left her parents and went to live with actress Karen Black, a family friend. She then dropped out of high school.

Rush Limbaugh, multi-millionaire media mogul, the most popular radio talk show host ever, bestselling book author. Dropped out of college after being required to take ballroom dancing.

Abraham Lincoln, lawyer, U.S. president. Finished barely a year of formal schooling. He was self-taught trigonometry (for his work as a surveyor) and read Blackstone on his own to become a lawyer. Of the 44 people who served as president of the United States, 8 never went to college.

Charles Lindbergh, aviator, first person to fly solo across the Atlantic Ocean. Quit the University of Wisconsin after two years to learn how to fly an airplane.

Carl Lindner, billionaire investor, founder of United Dairy Farmers, former owner of Chiquita Brands. Dropped out of high school at the age of 14 to deliver milk for the family store during the Depression.

Blake Lively, actress. At the age of 16, she got her first major movie role in *The Sisterhood of the Traveling Pants*. She started acting in the Gossip Girl TV series right after high school. She has not yet attended college, but has expressed a strong desire to do so.

John Llewellyn, labor leader, president of the United Mine Workers. Dropped out of high school.

Hank Locklin, country singer. Never attended college.

Marcus Loew, multimillionaire founder of Loews movie theaters, co-founder of MGM Movie Studio. Dropped out of elementary school.

Lindsay Lohan, actress. Never finished high school.

Dan Lok, multi-millionaire business mentor, founder of Quick Turn Marketing. College dropout. His CreativitySucks website notes: *A former college dropout, Dan Lok transformed himself from a grocery bagger in a local supermarket to a multi-millionaire. Dan came to North America with little knowledge of the English language and few contacts. Today, Dan is one of the most sought-after business mentors on the Web, as well as a best-selling author. His reputation includes his title as the World's #1 Website Conversion Expert.*

His books include:

How to Publish Your Own Best-Selling eBook in 21 Days or Less Without Writing

The Niche Formula: How to Quickly and Easily Find Hidden Niche Markets You Can Profit from Now

Turn Knowledge into Money: How to Get Rich Selling Information - Even if You Hate to Write or Aren't an Expert on Anything

GATE KEY

<u>Turn Words into Cash: How to Write a Sales Letter That Will Make You Rich</u>

Jack London, bestselling novelist. Dropped out of high school to work. Later was admitted to the University of California, but left after one semester.

Julie London, singer, actress. Dropped out of high school.

Sophia Loren, aka Sofia Scicolone, Oscar-winning actress, author, model. Dropped out of elementary school.

Caity Lotz, actress, dancer, stuntwoman, model, singer. Has not gone to college. Started out as a background dancer for music videos and tours. As she noted, "After I stopped going to school, my life was changed forever."

Joe Louis, boxer. Dropped out of high school.

Nat Love, member of the National Cowboys of Color Hall of Fame, known as Deadwood Dick, one of the first American cowboys to write his autobiography. Born into slavery. After being emancipated, he won a horse in a raffle and headed west to become a cowboy.

Tom Love, billionaire founder of Love's Travel Stops. After dropping out of the University of Oklahoma, he and his wife opened a gas station in Watonga, Oklahoma. They later also opened a convenience store. They now operate more than 300 travel stops in 39 states.

Forrest Lucas, long-haul trucker, multi-millionaire founder of Lucas Oil Products, race team sponsor. Left home at the age of 15 to work for a small cattle ranch. When he was 21, he bought his first semi. He later formed a trucking company.

Luiz Inacio Lula da Silva, Brazilian president. With a fifth grade education only, he shined shoes on the streets of Sao Paulo as a kid, but later became a steelworker union leader.

Sidney Lumet, film director. Dropped out of Columbia University after one year.

Peder Lund, publisher of Paladin Press. Dropped out of Kenyon College and headed to Miami to join the fight against Castro. Later enlisted in the Army where he attended Officer Candidate School, jump school and Ranger training.

Dolph Lundgren, actor, model, bodyguard. Won the European karate championships in 1980 and 1981. He was then awarded a Fulbright scholarship to MIT, but he lost interest in college after he was hired to be a bodyguard for singer Grace Jones, who helped him build a career as a model and actor.

Barbara Lynch, chef, owner of a $10 million group of restaurants in Boston. Dropped out of high school to be a runner for local bookies. Later worked for celebrity chef, Todd English.

I started my first business venture in high school, placing bets for some of my teachers with bookies in Southie.... I never did homework. I was failing everything. Senior year, they said I would have to go to summer school. There was no way I was doing that, so I dropped out. – Chef English

Susan Lyne, journalist, editor in chief, Hollywood executive, multimedia mogul. Never finished college at the University of California at Berkeley. As he noted, "The lure of taking a job in the grown-up world was greater."

Mary Lyon, education pioneer, teacher, founder of Mount Holyoke College (America's first women's college). Dropped out of high school. Started teaching at the age of 17.

Andie MacDowell, Golden Globe-winning actress and model. Dropped out of Winthrop College during her sophomore year.

John Mackey, founder of Whole Foods and developer of Conscious Capitalism. Dropped out of the University of Texas six times. Never took a business course.

Harry Macklowe, billionaire real estate developer. Dropped out of college to become a real estate broker.

Steve Madden, shoe designer. Dropped out of college to sell shoes on Long Island.

Ivory Madison, comic book author and founder of the Red Room social network for authors. Dropped out of school at the age of 13. Eventually went to law school without finishing high school or attending college.

John Major, British prime minister. High school dropout.

Jo Malone, multimillionaire founder of Jo Malone and Jo Loves cosmetology companies. She left school at the age of 14 after her mother had a nervous breakdown, so she could take care of her mother and younger sister. Never attended college.

Howie Mandel, comedian, game show host. Was expelled from Toronto's Northview Heights secondary school for practical jokes gone too far. Finally got his GED in 2010.

Henning Mankell, author of 40 books. At the age of 16, he made a decision to go to the university of life. He left school and traveled for Paris to become a writer. During the next few years, he worked at a musical instrument shop, a merchant marine ship, and an African theater company.

Leslie Mann, actress and comedienne. After high school, she took a number of acting classes with Joanne Baron and then studied with the Groundlings improv troupe. Did not attend college.

David Marcus, founder of mobile payment company Zong, CEO of Paypal. Dropped out of the University of Geneva to work at a bank to help support his family.

Isaac Marion, author of *Warm Bodies* novel, installer of heating ducts, guard of power plants, supervisor of parental visits for foster children, etc. Did not attend college.

Bruno Mars, singer, songwriter, music producer. After graduating from high school, he moved to Los Angeles and signed with Motown Records. He later wrote songs for other singers and released a bestselling record with Elektra.

Dean Martin, singer, actor, comedian. Never finished high school.

Steve Martin, comedian, actor. Dropped out of Long Beach State College. He became disillusioned upon reading Wittgenstein's view that "all philosophical problems can be reduced to problems of semantics."

Craig Martineau, co-founder of EcoScraps. Dropped out of Brigham Young University to pursue his composting business.

Manuel Marulanda, aka Pedro Antonio Marin, leader of the revolutionary Armed Forces of Colombia (FARC). The son of a peasant farmer, he had only a sixth-grade education.

Andrew Mason, co-founder of Groupon. Was offered $1 million by his partner to quit college and begin working on the daily deal website.

Konosuke Matsushita, multimillionaire founder of Panasonic. At the age of 10, he was apprenticed to a hibachi store in Osaka, Japan.

Robert Maxwell, billionaire publisher. Dropped out of high school.

John Mayer, Grammy-winning singer and songwriter. Left the Berklee College of Music after two semesters to pursue a singing career in Atlanta, Georgia. "I've already won one of the biggest gambles of all time, which was to forgo an education so I could pursue a real all-or-none scenario."

Martina McBride, country music singer. After high school, she traveled around Kansas playing and singing with various bands. Did not attend college.

Jenny McCarthy, actress and talk show host. A college dropout.

Melissa McCarthy, actress. Dropped out of Southern Illinois University at the age of 20 to move to New York City where she tried stand-up comedy for six months. Then did off-Broadway plays. Finally moved to Los Angeles to act.

Craig McCaw, billionaire founder of McCaw Cellular. Dropped out of college.

Billy Joe (Red) McCombs, billionaire founder of Clear Channel media empire, car dealerships, real estate investor. Dropped out of law school to sell cars in 1950. He owned his first automobile dealership by the age of 25.

Alexander McQueen, clothing designer. Was apprenticed at the age of 16 to Anderson & Sheppard tailors. Never attended college.

Steve McQueen, actor. Left reform school at the age of 16. Did many odd jobs before joining the Marines. Used the GI bill to study acting at Sanford Meisner's Neighborhood Playhouse. Never attended college.

Leighton Meester, actress and model. Dropped out of high school after her junior year (but had enough credits to get her diploma). Moved to New York City at the age of 10 to start a career as a model. When she was 14, she moved to Los Angeles to pursue a career as an actress.

I was very passionate about pursuing my acting career; as opposed to the daily routine of high school, which bored me to death. It was a chore - I wasn't in any after-school clubs. The only thing I did after school was go to auditions. (*Seventeen* Magazine)

Hendrik Meijer, founder of Meijer grocery stores. Worked as a barber during the depression. Did not attend college.

Herman Melville, novelist, *Moby Dick*. High school dropout.

Karl Menninger, psychiatrist. Dropped out of Washburn College in Kansas after two years.

Ron Meyer, talent agent, co-founder of CAA, executive at Universal Studios. Did two years in the Marines after dropping out of University and Venice High Schools. Started as a messenger at an agency before becoming an agent himself.

Bret Michaels, rock singer, reality TV show star. Graduated high school with a GED degree. Has not attended college.

Jillian Michaels, fitness expert, reality TV star, book author. She dropped out of California State University at Northridge to be a bartender. When her boyfriend suggested she get a real job, she faked a college diploma to get a position at the ICM talent agency.

Alyson "Aly" Michalka, actress, singer, songwriter (part of the duo Aly &AJ, now known as 78violet). Has not yet attended college.

Amanda Joy "AJ" Michalka, model, actress, singer, songwriter (part of the duo Aly &AJ, now known as 78violet). Has not yet attended college.

Lea Michele, singer, actress. After high school, she worked on Broadway. A few years later, she landed in Los Angeles and soon landed a role on Glee TV show. Has not attended college.

James Middleton, founder of a cake kit company, brother of Kate Middleton of England. Dropped out of college.

Cesar Millan, the dog whisperer and reality TV show star. Has not attended college.

Ben Milne, founder of Dwolla, a web-based payment network. Dropped out of the University of Northern Iowa during his freshman year to design audio speakers and sell them online.

Nicki Minaj, aka Onika Tanya Maraj, singer and songwriter. After graduating from high school, she worked as a waitress and other odd jobs while trying to land a record deal. She finally got her break after being featured in an underground rap DVD.

Liza Minnelli, Oscar-winning actress, singer. High school dropout.

Hellen Mirren, Oscar-winning actress. Left home at the age of 17 to go to London to become a professional actress. Did not attend college.

Robert Mitchum, actor. High school dropout.

Moby, author, rock star, tea-shop proprietor. Sold more than 15 million albums. A college dropout.

Art Modell, NFL football team owner, Baltimore Ravens. A high school dropout.

Nirav Modi, billionaire jeweler. Dropped out of Wharton to work with his uncle in India.

Michael Moore, documentary filmmaker, book author. Never attended college. "I have a high school education."

Claude Monet, painter. Elementary school dropout.

Marilyn Monroe, aka Norma Jeane Baker, actress, greatest blonde of all time (according to at least one poll). Left high school to marry James Dougherty (primarily to avoid going back to an orphanage). Became one of the best comic actresses of all time. Never finished high school.

Gene Montesano, co-founder of Lucky Brands jeans and Civilianaire clothing. Started working at a retail clothing store at the age of 19. Never attended college.

Arthur Ernest Morgan, flood control engineer, book author, college president, director of the Tennessee Valley Authority. Left high school after three years. Later attended the University of Colorado for six weeks.

Heather Morris, dancer, singer, actress. Dropped out of Arizona State University after two semesters to pursue a dancing career in Los Angeles.

Ed Morrisey, blogger at Captain's Quarters and HotAir.com. "I never finished college. I attended three or four different colleges at different times for different reasons. I never did get a degree."

GATE KEY

Chris Morrison, co-founder of PLP Digital Systems (software company). Earns more than $500,000 per year. Dropped out of high school.

Matthew Morrison, actor and singer. Attended New York University for two years before landing a role in the Broadway production of *Footloose*.

Dustin Moskovitz, billionaire co-founder of Facebook social network. Dropped out of Harvard.

Kate Moss, multi-millionaire model. Attended a little bit of college, but never graduated.

Wolfgang Amadeus Mozart, classical music composer and performer. In his early years, his father taught him music, languages and other academic subjects. From the age of 6, he performed along with his older sister in cities all over Europe. He never attended high school or college.

Charlotte Kemp Muhl, singer, songwriter, model, member of the Ghost of a Saber Tooth Tiger group. Moved to New York City alone at the age of 14 to become a model. Has not yet attended college.

Matt Mullenweg, founder of WordPress. Dropped out of the University of Houston to take a job at CNET Networks. Later co-founded WordPress.

Charles Munger, billionaire right-hand man to Warren Buffett in Berkshire Hathaway. Dropped out of the University of Michigan to join the Air Force as a meteorologist. Later got a law degree from Harvard.

David Murdock, billionaire investor, real estate tycoon, chairman of Dole Foods. Funding a $1.5 billion health research campus in North Carolina. Dropped out of high school in the 9th grade. Worked at a gas station until he was drafted into the Army in 1943.

Justin Murdock, investor, son of David. A college dropout and Goth musician.

Bobby Murphy, early employee at Snapchat. Dropped out of Stanford to work on Snapchat.

Ted Murphy, founder, Izea Entertainment, social media marketing company. Dropped out of Florida State University to start Think Creative ad agency.

Bill Murray, Golden Globe-winning actor, comedian. Dropped out of Regis University after being arrested for possession of marijuana.

Stan Musial, Hall of Fame baseball player. Turned down a college scholarship to pitch for a minor league baseball team.

Elon Musk, founder of Paypal, founder of SpaceX, founder of Tesla Motors, founder of SolarCity, software engineer, entrepreneur. Graduated from Penn with a double major. Enrolled in a PhD program at Stanford University, but dropped out after two days. As he has noted, "I find universities a very slow place to learn things."

George Naddaff, founder of Boston Chicken and UFood Grill. Never attended college. As he put it, "School and I did not work out. So at age 17 and a half, I joined the Army." And, when he got out of the Army, his dad said if you're not going to college, you get a job. He did. The next day.

Walter Nash, prime minister of New Zealand. Dropped out of high school.

David Neeleman, founder of JetBlue airlines. Dropped out of the University of Utah after three years.

Jack Nelson, Pulitzer Prize winning journalist. Never attended college. After high school, he went to work for the Biloxi Daily Herald. Later he opened the Atlanta bureau of the *Los Angeles Times* and later became the *Times* bureau chief in Washington, D.C.

Richard John Neuhaus, theologian, Lutheran minister, Catholic priest, author, civil rights activist. He took pride in the fact that he never graduated from high school.

Donald Newhouse, billionaire publisher, Advanced Publications. Dropped out of Syracuse University.

Jim Newton, founder of TechShop (the nation's first full-service gym for the tinkering crowd), science advisor for Discovery Channel's *MythBusters* series. Dropped out of college.

Olivia Newton-John, singer, actress, author. Dropped out of high school.

Jake Nickell, cofounder and CEO of Treadless.com. Never graduated from college.

Xavier Niel, computer programmer, Internet billionaire, chairman of Free Mobile and Kima Ventures venture capital firm. No college degree.

Connie Nielsen, actress. Left Denmark at 18 to pursue a career as an actress. Has not attended college.

Florence Nightingale, nurse. No formal education. Home schooled.

Kristi Noem, U.S. representative. Dropped out of college to carry on her dad's farm after he died in a farm-based accident. 20 years later, she finally graduated from college (while carrying on a full-time role as a congresswoman for South Dakota).

Sinead O'Connor, singer. Never attended college.

Rosie O'Donnell, comedienne, talk show host. Dropped out of Dickinson College and Boston University.

George Alan O'Dowd, aka Boy George, singer, songwriter, fashion designer, photographer. High school dropout. Never attended college.

GATE KEY

David Ogilvy, advertising copywriter and executive. Was thrown out of Oxford University at the age of 20 in 1931 during the Great Depression. Began working as a lowly cook in a hotel restaurant. Eventually became a world-class chef. Left that job to sell upmarket kitchen stoves, which led to a job in advertising.

Mark Oliari, co-owner of Coins 'N Things, the largest seller of gold to the U.S. government. After high school he went right into trading coins full-time and never looked back. Within a few years, his engineer father quit his job and joined his son.

Ashley Olsen, actress and fashion designer. Has not yet attended college.

Mary-Kate Olsen, actress and fashion designer. Has not yet attended college.

Jacqueline Kennedy Onassis, U.S. first lady, book editor. Dropped out of Vassar before eventually graduating from George Washington University.

Timmy O'Neill, climber, guide, comedian, percussionist, slack liner, mountain biker, class V paddler, BASE jumper, backcountry skier. Started climbing at the age of 19. Did not graduate from college.

Yoko Ono, artist, singer. Dropped out of Sarah Lawrence College.

David Oreck, multimillionaire founder of The Oreck Corporation that builds those wonderful vacuum cleaners. When the U.S. entered World War II, he quit college to enlist in the Army Air Corps. After the war, college seemed to tame to him, so he started working as a salesman at a Manhattan appliance distributor. That job eventually led him to founding his own company.

Amancio Ortega, fashion retailer, Spain's richest man, billionaire. Dropped out of high school at the age of 14 to run errands for mom-and-pop shirt stores.

George Orwell (aka Eric Blair), author of *Animal Farm* and *1984*. Instead of attending university after graduating from Eton, he joined the Imperial Police and worked in Burma. When he returned, he worked in restaurant kitchens, slept in homeless shelters and eventually documented the condition of miners. All the time, he was writing reviews, essays, novels, and a regular newspaper column. His *Animal Farm* has sold more than 10 million copies.

Aimee Osbourne, actress, singer. Did not finish high school.

Jack Osbourne, music manager, reality TV star. Did not finish high school.

John Michael "Ozzy" Osbourne, heavy metal singer, songwriter, and reality TV star. Left school at the age of 15.

Kelly Osbourne, reality TV star, actress, singer, fashion designer. Did not finish high school.

Joel Osteen, TV pastor and host of the most-watched inspirational TV show in the U.S. Dropped out of Oral Roberts University after one year to care for his mother (who was recovering from cancer). Has sold more than 4 million copies of *Your Best Life Now*.

Fred Otash, celebrity detective. Left home to join the Marines before joining the Los Angeles police department. Later became a detective to Hollywood celebrities.

Dan Panoz, founder of Panoz Auto Development car design firm. Dropped out of Embry-Riddle Aeronautical University and Gainesville College.

Larry Page, billionaire co-founder of Google. Dropped out of the Stanford Ph.D. program in computer science to start Google in 1998 working out of a friend's garage. Unlike Brian, he never returned to finish the Ph.D. program.

Patti Page, aka Clara Ann Fowler, singer. As a teen, she took a job in the art department of KTUL radio. Never attended college.

Charlie "Bird" Parker, jazz musician and father of modern jazz. Attended Lincoln High School in Kansas City, Missouri, but left after a year and a half to join the local musicians' union.

Sean Parker, billionaire co-creator of Napster, founding president of Facebook.com. He barely finished high school (he was not interested in school). Never made it to college. "I kind of refer to it as Napster University. It was a crash course in intellectual property law, corporate finance, entrepreneurship and law school."

"Formal education becomes less and less important. We should expect to see the emergence of a new kind of entrepreneur who has acquired most of their knowledge through self-exploration" (quoted in *The Education of Millionaires* by Michael Ellsberg).

Rosa Parks, civil rights pioneer. Dropped out of high school.

Adam Passey, vice president of information and technology for a marketing agency. Then hired by IGN Entertainment. Never graduated from college.

Danica Patrick, race car driver. Instead of going to high school, she went to London when she was 16 to train as a driver (and where she got her GED). She has not yet attended college.

Aaron Paul, actor, *Breaking Bad*.

Kevin Paul, founder of KPaul, an Inc. 500 company. Joined the army straight out of high school. Never attended college.

Jeno Paulucci, multi-millionaire founder of Chun King and Jeno's. Left school at the age of 16 to sell fruits and vegetables. Twenty years later he borrowed $2,500 to begin canning his own version of chow mein. He sold Chun King 11 years later for $63 million. Several years later, he founded Jeno's where he created pizza rolls. He sold that company 17 years later for $140 million.

Harvey Pekar, comic book author. Dropped out of Case Western Reserve University. His reason? He quit "when the pressure of required math classes proved too much to bear."

Nelson Peltz, billionaire leveraged buyout investor. Dropped out of Wharton Business School.

Pinetop Perkins, blues pianist. Left school after the third grade.

Andrew Perlman, co-founder of GreatPoint. Dropped out of Washington University to start an Internet communications company, Cignal Global Communications, when he was 19.

Barry Perlman, co-founder of Lucky Brands jeans and Civilianaire clothing. Opened his first retail clothing store at the age of 17. Never attended college.

Katy Perry, singer. Left home at the age of 14 to make it on her own in Nashville; then moved to Los Angeles at the age of 17. Did not attend college. Worked various crappy jobs and sank into debt until she signed a deal with Capitol Records and released her bestselling album, *One of the Boys*.

John Pestana, multimillionaire co-founder of Omniture. Dropped out of Brigham Young University during his final semester to co-found MyComputer.com, which became Omniture.

Todd Phillips, screenwriter, director, and producer, Green Hat Films. Dropped out of film school at New York University to promote his first documentary, *Hatred*.

George Phippen, artist, cofounder of Cowboy Artists of America. "Quituated" school before the eighth grade.

Joaquin Phoenix, actor, director, producer, singer. Did not attend college.

River Phoenix, actor, singer, songwriter. Did not attend college.

Phosphorescent, country singer. Left home at 18 to tour the Southwest. Lived out of his pickup for six months.

Pablo Picasso, modern artist, painter, sculptor, co-founder of Cubism, co-inventor of collage. At the age of 16, he attended the Royal Academy of San Fernando (Spain's foremost art school), but he disliked the formal instruction and soon quit attending classes altogether.

Mary Pickford, Oscar-winning actress, co-founder of United Artists. Six months of formal education. Home schooled.

GATE KEY

James A. Pike, Episcopal bishop. Dropped out of the University of Santa Clara after his sophomore year.

François Pinault, third-richest man in France, owner of Gucci, Samsonite, Puma, and Christie's auctions. Quit high school to work at his father's lumber mill.

Brad Pitt, actor. Left the University of Missouri two credits short of graduating so he could begin his acting career in California.

Sidney Poitier, Oscar-winning actor. Only finished a few grades. Could only read at the fourth-grade level until a friend taught him how to read better when he was a struggling actor in New York City.

Sydney Pollack, movie director, producer, and actor. Skipped college and enrolled at the Neighborhood Playhouse, where he studied under drama coach Sanford Meisner.

Eugene Polley, inventor of the wireless remote control. Attended the City Colleges of Chicago and the Armour Institute of Technology (now the Illinois Institute of Technology), but did not have enough money to graduate from college. Joined Zenith as a parts clerk at the age of 20 and rose from the stockroom to the engineering department based on his mechanical aptitude. Eventually earned 18 U.S. patents for his inventions.

Ron Popeil, multimillionaire founder of Ronco, inventor, infomercial pitchman and producer. Dropped out of college. He did receive the Ig Nobel

Award, though, for Consumer Engineering. Inventor of the Solid Flavor Injector, Mr. Microphone, Showtime Rotisserie and more.

Joe Poulin, founder of Luxury Retreats, started developing websites when he was a teen. Flew to Barbados to build a website for a local villa rental group. That, in turn, led to his starting Luxury Retreats. Has not attended college.

William Powell, author of *The Anarchist Cookbook*. Dropped out of high school. Later applied to attend Windham College, but did not spend much time there. Eventually he did earn a master's degree in English and taught school for many years.

William J. Powell, developer and owner of the Clearview Golf Club, the first U.S. golf course designed, owned and operated by an African American; also competed in the first U.S. interracial collegiate golf match. Left Wilberforce University early because he had an enlarged heart.

Azim Premji, chairman of Wipro. Dropped out of Stanford University to rush home to India to take care of his family after his father died. Built Wipro into a multibillion company. Many years later he completed his Stanford degree via correspondence course. "If my father had not died, I probably would have stayed in the U.S. and completed my master's degree."

Lisa Marie Presley, singer. Dropped out of high school.

GATE KEY

Seth Priebatsch, chief of SCVNGR.com and founder of PostcardTech. Dropped out of Princeton University after one year.

Jeff Probst, host, *Survivor* TV show. Dropped out of college after three and a half years to pursue a career as a singer in a rock 'n roll band.

Bob Proctor, success speaker, bestselling author of *You Were Born Rich*, teacher of *The Secret*, and co-founder of Life Success Publishing. Went to high school for two months.

Wolfgang Puck, chef, owner of 16 restaurants and 80 express bistros. Quit school at the age of 14 and got a job as a cooking apprentice at a hotel. When he told his father, he said, "Well, you're good for nothing. Cooking is for women."

Ian Purkayastha, prince of truffles, North American sales director for PAQ. Dropped out of Baruch College during orientation week. Has not yet gone back to college.

David Putnam, Oscar-winning producer. Dropped out of high school.

Ernie Pyle, journalist. Left high school early to become a cub reporter.

Dennis Quaid, actor. Dropped out of the University of Houston to pursue an acting career in Hollywood.

Ashley Qualls, founder of Whateverlife.com, left high school at the age of 15 to devote full time to her website business where she made more than a million dollars by the age of 17.

Aidan Quinn, actor. Did not attend college. Was a roofer by trade before getting his start as an actor at the age of 19.

Anthony Quinn, Oscar-winning actor. Dropped out of high school.

Lew Ranieri, financier, the father of mortgage-backed bonds. Dropped out of college.

Royal Richard "Jim" Rathman, race-car driver. Never attended college. Became a renowned drag racer while still a teenager, receiving 48 traffic tickets before he was 18. Took the name of his older brother Jim so he could compete in major races at the age of 20 (claiming to be the age of his brother at 24).

James Arthur Ray, inspirational author and speaker. Dropped out of junior college to work as a telemarketer.

Rachael Ray, TV chef, cookbook author. Dropped out of Pace University after two years to work and save money.

Usher Raymond IV, quadruple platinum singer. He won the *Star Search* male teen vocalist competition when he was 18. He was signed to a music label immediately thereafter.

GATE KEY

Robert Redford, actor, producer, director, founder of the Sundance Institute. He was booted from the University of Colorado after three semesters for drinking too much. Then spent a year in France trying to become a success as a painter. Returned to New York where he studied drama and landed his first acting role in the theater.

Keanu Reeves, actor. He dropped out of high school to pursue acting.

Kamilla Reid, book author. A high school dropout.

Lynda Resnick, billionaire co-founder of POM Wonderful. A child actress, Lynda dropped out of college to start an advertising agency at the age of 19. She and her husband are one of the country's largest producers of pomegranates, pistachios and mandarin oranges.

Burt Reynolds, actor, number-one box office attraction for five straight years (1978-82). Dropped out of Florida State University after football and automobile accident injuries ended his football career. Then took some classes at Palm Beach Junior College where his teacher pushed Reynolds into acting.

Dane Reynolds, world class surfer, video documentarian. Dropped out of school at the age of 16 to surf, something he called "kind of a stupid decision."

Ryan Reynolds, actor. Moved to Los Angeles at the age of 19 to become an actor. Never attended college.

Trent Rezner, musician, Nine Inch Nails. Dropped out of Allegheny College after one year to pursue a career in music.

Charlie Rich, Grammy-winning country and blues singer and songwriter. Dropped out of the University of Arkansas to join the Air Force.

Marc Rich, billionaire commodities investor, built Philbro into the world's largest commodities firm, founded Marc Rich & Co. Dropped out of NYU to take a job in the mail room of Philipp Brothers on Wall Street.

Rihanna, aka Robyn Rihanna Fenty, singer, actress. At the age of 15, she formed a singing trio in Barbados. At the age of 16, she went to live with songwriter Evan Rogers and his wife in Connecticut. At the age of 17, she signed a singing contract with Def Jam records. Has not yet attended college.

Kelly Ripa, actress and talk show host. Moved to New York City at the age of 19 to pursue a career as an actress. Did not attend college. "I always wanted to be a teacher. I just didn't have the devotion to go to school."

Krysten Ritter, model and actress. Was spotted by a model agent at the age of 15 (while shopping in a Pennsylvania mall). Started modeling that next summer at the age of 16. Moved to New York after high school to model in commercials. Has never attended college.

GATE KEY

Leandro Rizzuto, billionaire founder of Conair. Dropped out of college to found Conair with a $100 investment and the invention of a hot-air hair roller.

Emma Roberts, actress. Because of her work schedule as a young actress, she switched to being home-schooled. As she noted, "My friends joke that I've only been to high school in a movie." She has been accepted at Sarah Lawrence College, but has not yet attended.

Julia Roberts, actress. After high school, she headed to New York City where she pursued an acting career (while selling shoes and working at an ice cream stand). Has never attended college.

Pernell Roberts, actor (*Bonanza* and *Trapper John*). Attended Georgia Tech and the University of Maryland, but at both schools, as he noted, "I distinguished myself by flunking out."

Britt Robertson, actress. Home-schooled. In her early teens, she moved to Los Angeles to pursue a career as an actress. Has not attended college.

Andrew Robl, millionaire online poker player. Started playing poker during high school, but turned professional after the second semester of his freshman year at the University of Michigan.

Nevaldo Rocha, billionaire founder of the Guararapes Confeccoes fashion empire. Never attended high school.

Chris Rock, comedian, actor. Dropped out of high school.

John D. Rockefeller Sr., billionaire founder of Standard Oil, philanthropist. History's first recorded billionaire. Dropped out of high school two months before graduation. Took some courses at a local business school.

Dorothy Rodham, mother of Hillary Rodham Clinton. Her mother had promised to fund her college education, but then reneged on the commitment, so she never attended college.

Michelle Rodriguez, actress. Was expelled from five different schools during high school (for fighting and for questioning her teachers). She dropped out of high school, but later earned her GED. Briefly attended business school before quitting to pursue her career as an actress. Never attended college.

Seth Rogan, actor, comedian, and screenwriter. Dropped out of high school.

Roy Rogers, aka Leonard Slye, singing cowboy, actor. Dropped out of high school. As he noted, I did pretty well "for a guy who never finished high school and used to yodel at square dances."

Will Rogers, humorist, author, actor, entertainer. High school dropout.

Kjell Inge Rokke, billionaire Norwegian businessman. No secondary or college education. Started out as a fisherman at the age of 18.

Ray Romano, actor, *Everybody Loves Raymond*. Went to college for seven years, but never graduated. "I would get my student loans, get money, register and never really go. It was a system I thought would somehow pan out."

Rebecca Romijn, actress, model. Deferred her studies at the University of California at Santa Cruz to pursue a modeling career in Paris, France.

George Romney, automotive executive, Michigan governor, presidential candidate. Spent only a year at the University of Utah.

Kevin Rose, founder of Digg.com, TechTV host. Dropped out of the University of Las Vegas during his sophomore year to code software. He wrote his first software program in the second grade and was building his own machines by the beginning of high school. He started Digg with $1,200 and launched the site out of his bedroom.

Barney Rosset, book and magazine publisher, film producer and distributor. Dropped out of several colleges. Then served as an Army photographer in China during World War II.

Alexander Rossi, motorsports driver. Graduated high school at the age of 16 to pursue a full-time career as a driver. Has not attended college.

Renzo Rosso, billionaire co-founder of Diesel jeans. Joined Italian fashion manufacturer Moltex at the age of 20, owned 40% of the business by the age of 22. Renamed the company Diesel in 1978.

Emmy Rossum, actress, singer. Attended Columbia University for half a semester. But, then dove headlong into acting in three movies.

Asher Roth, hip hop artist, *I Love College* hit song. Dropped out of West Chester University after being signed.

André René Roussimoff, aka André the Giant, wrestler and actor. Dropped out of school after the 8th grade.

Karl Rove, presidential advisor. Left the University of Utah after two years to work for the college Republicans.

Kelly Rowland, singer. Has not yet attended college. "I wanted to be a psychiatrist, but I made my first million at 18 years old. That's when I figured I would do well enough for myself."

Frederick Henry Royce, multimillionaire co-founder of Rolls-Royce, automotive designer. Elementary school dropout.

Michael Rubin, billionaire founder of e-commerce company GSI Commerce and Kynetic (including ShopRunner, Rue La La, and Fanatics). Dropped out of Villanova University after six months to open several retail ski shops.

He admits, "If I had to do it over again, I would have gone to college. I missed out on that. The business responsibilities weighted hard on me in my late teens and early 20s."

Phillip Ruffin, billionaire casino operator. He dropped out of Wichita State to flip burgers. With the money he saved, he invested in convenience stores, oil and real estate. Eventually he got into casinos. The best day of his life? August 10, 2007. The day he put $1.24 billion into his checking account.

"The advice I would give to young people? Quit your job. Don't work for anybody. You really can't make any money working for someone else" (quoted in *The Education of Millionaires* by Michael Ellsberg).

Jane Russell, actress. Howard Hughes discovered her when she was 19 and cast her in the Western, *The Outlaw*. She did not attend college.

Leon Russell, aka Charles Russell Bridges, singer, rock musician. Moved to Los Angeles, California from Oklahoma at the age of 17. Never attended college.

Rene Russo, model, actress. After a year at Burroughs High School in Burbank, California, she dropped out. At the age of 17, she took a job inspecting lenses in an eyeglass factory, but was soon discovered by a model agent.

Haim Saban, billionaire producer of the Mighty Morphin Power Rangers TV show. He also owns stakes in Univision and Paul Frank Industries. He never attended college.

William Safire, columnist for the *New York Times*. Dropped out of Syracuse University to take a job as a researcher for a column.

Edmond Safra, billionaire banker, philanthropist. High school dropout.

J.D. Salinger, novelist, *Catcher in the Rye* (with over 60 million copies sold so far). Briefly attended Ursinus College and New York University before publishing short stories in *Collier's* and *Esquire*.

Colonel Harlan Sanders, multimillionaire founder of Kentucky Fried Chicken (KFC). Elementary school dropout, but later earned a law degree via correspondence course.

Sankaralingam, social and political reformer, founder of Land for Tiller's Freedom. A member of the high caste in India, he quit college to join Gandhi's movement for India's freedom.

Silvio Santos, billionaire TV host, the first-ever Brazilian celebrity billionaire. Started out as a street vendor in Rio de Janeiro. Apparently did not attend college.

Jose Saramago, Nobel Prize-winning novelist. Graduated from trade school and then studied literature mostly on his own.

Brandon Sargent, co-founder of EcoScraps. Dropped out of Brigham Young University to pursue his composting business.

Cherilyn Sarkisian, aka Cher, singer, Oscar-winning actress. Dropped out of high school in the 11th grade and started taking acting lessons. At 16, she moved out of her house. Soon she met Sonny Bono and they formed Sonny and Cher, created many hits and starred in *The Sonny and Cher Comedy Hour*.

David Sarnoff, radio and TV producer. High school dropout.

William Saroyan, Oscar-winning screenwriter, Pulitzer Prize-winning playwright. High school dropout.

Vidal Sassoon, multimillionaire founder of Vidal Sassoon hairstyling salons and hair-care products. High school dropout.

Micah Schaffer, director of operations at Snapchat. Has not yet attended college.

Al Schneider, founder of Schneider National freight company. Had an eighth-grade education.

Maria Schneider, actress. Left home at the age of 15 to pursue a career as a model. At the age of 19, she was cast in the movie, *Last Tango in Paris*.

Nick Schorsch, billionaire founder of American Realty Capital Properties. Dropped out of college. Never returned to finish.

Richard Schulze, billionaire founder of Best Buy. After high school and the Air National Guard, he sold electronics for his father's distribution company and later opened a car-stereo shop. He never attended college.

Ryan Seacrest, multimillionaire radio and TV host. He turned a high school internship at a local radio station into his own show. At 19, he dropped out of the University of Georgia and headed to Hollywood to build a career in radio and TV.

Seal, aka Seal Henry Olusugun Olumide Adeola Samuel, R&B singer and songwriter. He received a two-year associate's degree in architecture. He struck out on his own at the age of 15.

Ke$ha Rose Sebert, singer and songwriter. She quit high school weeks before graduating and passed on a scholarship to Barnard College to go to Los Angeles to break into the music business.

Kyra Sedgwick, actress. She briefly attended Sarah Lawrence College and the University of Southern California before dropping out to act full time.

GATE KEY

Tom Selleck, actor. He left USC three classes short of a degree to become a contract player for 20th Century Fox. "I started out at about $35 a week, so it was a pretty big risk to leave college to do that. But, it's like my dad always said: "Risk is the price you pay for opportunity."

Doug Selsam, inventor of The Sky Serpent wind generator and heavy metal guitarist. He attended the University of California at Irvine, but never graduated.

Drew Sementa, founder, Premier Payment Systems. He left the University of Central Florida after his junior year to join a dot-com.

Maurice Sendak, bestselling children's book author and illustrator. He never attended college. He had a number of odd jobs before landing a job as a window dresser at the FAO Schwartz toy store in New York City. His first book illustrations were published when he was 19 years old.

Amanda Seyfried, actress. She walked out of Fordham University on her first day of classes in 2004. As she notes, "You can learn more on your own."

William Shakespeare, playwright, poet. He had only a few years of formal schooling.

Shakira, aka Shakira Isabel Mebarak Ripoll, Grammy-winning singer and songwriter who has sold more than 50 million albums. She attended a modeling school for a time. While she never attended college, she founded Pies Descalzos to provide educational opportunities to thousands of Colombia's poorest children and Barefoot, a nonprofit organization to provide schooling opportunities for millions of children around the world.

Adam Shankman, dancer, choreographer, director, producer, reality show judge. He dropped out of Julliard to return to Los Angeles to pursue a choreography career.

George Bernard Shaw, playwright, author. High school dropout.

Charlie Sheen, actor. Never finished high school.

Martin Sheen (Ramon Gerard Estevez), actor. Never attended college until he went for a few months in 2006.

Blake Shelton, country singer, reality competition panelist. Left home right after high school and went to Nashville to try to make it as a country singer. Never attended college.

Robert Sherman, Oscar-winning songwriter. At the age of 17, he enlisted in the Army. After World War II, he returned to write a novel, but was soon encouraged to partner with his brother Richard in writing songs.

J. Earl Shoaff, the Millionaire Maker. Never graduated from high school.

GATE KEY

Walter Shorenstein, billionaire real estate investor, Shorenstein Properties. Dropped out of the University of Pennsylvania. Began buying commercial property after serving in the military during World War II.

Alan Sillitoe, novelist. He left school at the age of 14 to work in a bicycle plant.

Russell Simmons, multi-millionaire co-founder of Def Jam records, founder Russell Simmons Music Group, creator of Phat Farm and Baby Phat fashions, founding partner of UniRush Financial Services, creator of Global Grind website, bestselling author, movie and TV producer. Left City College of New York at the age of 20 to begin promoting local rap music acts (which he eventually signed to his music label) and producing records.

Maggy Simony, author of *Traveler's Reading Guide*. Never attended college.

John Simplot, billionaire potato king. Dropped out of 8th grade and left home at the age of 14. He sorted potatoes and raised hogs before saving enough money to buy his first potato field. Became a millionaire by the age of 30.

Ashley Simpson, actress and singer. When she turned 18, she moved out of her parent's house. Has not yet attended college.

Jessica Simpson, singer and actress. Left high school at the age of 16 to pursue a singing career. Later got her GED. Never attended college.

Frank Sinatra, singer, Oscar-winning actor. Never finished high school.

Isaac Merrit Singer, sewing machine inventor, multimillionaire founder of Singer Industries. Dropped out of elementary school.

Derek Silvers, founder of CD Baby and MuckWork, professional musician, entrepreneur. Attended Berklee College of Music for three years, but it is not clear if he graduated or not (he's very sparse with his online biographies).

"The unquestioned college path deserves to be challenged." - Derek Silvers

Alexander Skarsgård, actor, director. After high school, he did national service in an anti-terrorism unit. He then attended Leeds Metropolitan University in England for six months, but didn't study much. Instead, he "had a blast." He later took a theater course at Marymount Manhattan College before continuing to pursue his acting career.

Christian Slater, actor. Dropped out of high school and moved to Los Angeles to pursue a career in acting.

Alfred E. Smith, governor of New York and presidential candidate. Left school at the age of 14 to help his family after his father died. He would later joke that he received his FFM degree from the Fulton Fish Market in New York City.

GATE KEY

Daniel Smith, early employee at Snapchat. Dropped out of Stanford to work on Snapchat.

Dylan Smith, multi-millionaire co-founder of Box.net. Dropped out of Duke University and headed to Silicon Valley to build the business.

Elinor Smith, aviatrix, the Flying Flapper. By the time she was 17, she was ferrying passengers on short hops from Roosevelt Field in Long Island. By 18, she had her own sight-seeing business. Never attended college.

O. Bruton Smith, billionaire. "I didn't attend college, but still had a good time. I think I probably had more fun than any human deserves a right to have."

Patti Smith, poet, visual artist, songwriter. Dropped out of teacher's college to start life as an artist in New York City.

Ryan Smith, chief marketing officer, Qualtrics. He was two credits shy of an undergraduate degree at Brigham Young University when he quit to work for his family's business.

Walter L. Smith, president of Florida A&M University. Dropped out of high school, but later earned an equivalency diploma at the age of 23.

Will Smith, Grammy-winning rapper, actor. Did not attend college. As the Fresh Prince, he and DJ Jazzy Jeff released their first album before he finished high school. They received the first Grammy for a hip-hop act. Due to the success of that first album, Smith decided to forego college for show business.

The things that have been most valuable to me I did not learn in school. Traditional education is based on facts and figures and passing tests — not on a comprehension of the material, and its application to your life. ... I know how to learn anything I want to learn. ... Give me the book, and I do not need somebody to stand up in front of the class. — Will Smith

Edwin "Duke" Snider, Hall of Fame baseball player. Went into the military after high school and then signed a minor league baseball contract. Never attended college.

Phoebe Snow, singer, songwriter. Dropped out of college to perform in clubs and coffeehouses. Frank Sinatra said of her: "She is the best singer in the history of the world."

Daniel Snyder, billionaire owner of Snyder Communications and Red Zone Capital, owner of the Washington Redskins. Dropped out of the University of Maryland.

Josh Sommer, founder, Chordoma Foundation. Dropped out of Duke University to cofound the Chordoma Foundation to fund research on this rare bone cancer.

Kevin Sorbo, actor, director, producer, and model. Left Moorhead State University early to pursue a career in acting.

GATE KEY

Shannyn Sossamon, actress, dancer. Left her hometown of Reno, Nevada, the day after graduating high school. Headed to Los Angeles to pursue dance.

Angelo Sotira, multimillionaire founder of DMusic and deviantART. Founded DMusic while still in high school. Never attended college.

Kevin Spacey, actor, producer. Dropped out of Julliard after two years to act professionally.

James Spader, actor. Dropped out of high school. As he noted,

I left high school with the option of returning whenever I wanted. The high school was tremendously gracious in that way. They said, 'Any time you want to come back, we'll welcome you.' Maybe I should take them up on it. I'd probably make great use of it.

Britney Spears, singer, actress, youngest woman to have five albums debut at #1 on the Billboard list. Dropped out of high school.

Abigail Spencer, actress. Was discovered by a casting director while sitting in the audience of the *Regis & Kathie Lee* TV show (where they talked to her for a few seconds). She auditioned and was cast for a role in *All My Children*. Then, instead of going to Carnegie Mellon as she had planned, she moved to New York City to act. She has not attended college.

Evan Spiegel, co-founder of Snapchat. Dropped out of Stanford University a few weeks before graduation.

Steven Spielberg, billionaire movie director and producer, co-founder of DreamWorks. Rejected by the best film schools, he enrolled in and then dropped out of Cal State Long Beach. Received a degree in 2002.

Lysander Spooner, abolitionist, attorney and author. Did not attend college. In 1835, he challenged the law that kept those without college degrees from setting up as an attorney without five years of apprenticeship.

Rick Springfield, singer and actor. Never attended college.

Bruce Springsteen, Grammy-winning and Oscar-winning singer and songwriter. Never attended college.

Ringo Starr, drummer for the Beatles. He did not attend college.

Jason Statham, actor, model, diver. At the age of 15, he dropped out of school to work confidence games. Later dived for the British National Team. Became a model and then an actor.

Gwen Stefani, singer and songwriter, No Doubt. Struggled in school. Never attended college. "School was just really hard for me. I didn't want to fail. I wanted to be smart! But I was really dreaming. ... It makes me sad when I think about it. I still have nightmares about tests."

Jonathan "Jono" Steinberg, billionaire founder of Wisdom Tree Investments, dropped out of Wharton.

Jake Steinfeld, bodybuilder, founder of Body by Jake, co-founder of FitTV and Major League Lacrosse. Dropped out of the State University of New York and moved to California to follow his passion as a bodybuilder.

Greg Stemm, co-founder of Odyssey, a shipwreck recovery company. Studied marine biology for two years at New College of Florida before dropping out to work with Bob Hope as his PR man.

Dale Stephens, founder of Uncollege.org. Dropped out of Hendrix College for at least two years to launch Uncollege.org. Funded $100,000 by Peter Thiel, co-founder of Paypal via his college dropout project.

Hiram Stevens, engineer, inventor. Dropped out of high school.

Kristen Stewart, actress. Dropped out of school in the seventh grade to study independently at home. "That was a necessity. When I would go away to work, my teachers would only give me a portion of my schoolwork, and I would come home and they'd fail me. I was very happy to leave."

"I want to go to college for literature. I want to be a writer. I mean, I love what I do, but it's not all I want to do – be a professional liar for the rest of my life."

Patrick Stewart, actor, producer, director, writer. Dropped out of high school at the age of 15.

Ben Stiller, actor, director, and producer. Went to the UCLA film school for nine months and then headed for Broadway. As he noted, "I was the guy who dropped out and moved back in with his parents."

Dean Stockwell, actor and artist. Was a child movie star. Dropped out of acting at one point to work as a laborer. Never attended college.

Eric Stoltz, actor and producer. Dropped out of the University of Southern California in his junior year and joined a repertory acting company in Edinburgh, Scotland. Moved to New York City in 1981, studied with Stella Adler and Peggy Feury, and soon got his first film role in *Fast Times at Ridgemont High*.

Allen Stone, singer. Ditched Bible College to work as a musician.

Biz Stone, co-founder of Twitter and Obvious. A college dropout.

Emma Stone, actress. At the age of 15, she gave her parents a PowerPoint presentation about ditching high school to pursue a career as an actress. Her mother accompanied her to Hollywood so she could become an actress. She was home-schooled while auditioning for jobs. Has not yet attended college, but expressed interest in taking some classes after visiting the Salk Institute while filming *Spider-Man*.

GATE KEY

Edward D. Stone, architect. Dropped out of the University of Arkansas.

Sharon Stone, Golden Globe-winning and Emmy-winning actress, producer and model. Dropped out of Edinboro State University.

W. Clement Stone, multimillionaire insurance businessman, founder of *Success* Magazine, and author of a number of books on positive mental attitudes. At the age of six, he sold newspapers on the south side of Chicago. By the age of 13, he owned his own newsstand. He continued to work odd jobs until his mother bought a small insurance agency, where he helped her by selling insurance. At the age of 21, with $100 in his pocket, he established the Combined Registry Company insurance business which he built into a multi-million dollar business. He dropped out of elementary school, but later attended high school night courses and some college.

Tom Stoppart, Tony-winning playwright and Oscar-winning screenwriter. Didn't like school. Never attended college.

Madeleine Stowe, actress and screenwriter. Spent one year studying film and journalism at the University of Southern California. Never graduated from college.

Barbra Streisand, singer and actress. Started her singing career at the age of 18. Did not attend college.

Hilary Swank, actress, swimmer, gymnast. Dropped out of South Pasadena High School to act professionally. When she was 15, she and her mother headed to Los Angeles with $75 in their pockets. They lived out of their Oldsmobile Delta '88 until she found work in TV.

I did leave high school my sophomore year, but I got my GED. I wouldn't ever recommend not going to school. I think it's case by case. But what's really important is not just to have a diploma but also to experience life. I'm certainly not very book smart, but I started traveling at 16, and it has enriched me in ways I could never begin to explain. (Time Magazine)

"My education has been traveling the world, meeting different people and seeing all different walks of life." (*Ladies' Home Journal*)

Taylor Swift, singer and songwriter. Released her first album at the age of 16; left high school at the same age. Has not yet attended college.

Mark Sykes, art dealer, gambler, bookie, gentleman, and rogue. Attended Oxford University for 18 months (primarily running highly profitable card games) then dropped out to gamble professionally.

Louis Szekely, aka Louis C.K., comedian. Did not attend college. Instead, he worked at KFC, ran demolition for carpenters, fixed cars and worked in a video store.

GATE KEY

Jessica Szohr, model, actress. Graduated from high school a semester early and moved from Wisconsin to Los Angeles to work as a model, but she soon was cast in a number of TV shows. Has not attended college.

R.F. "Rawley" Taplett, founder of R.F. Taplett Fruit & Cold Storage Company, multi-millionaire investor. Had only a high school diploma.

Quentin Tarantino, movie director, producer and screenwriter. A high school dropout.

Benedikt Taschen, publisher of Taschen Books. At 18, he opened his first comic store. At 19, he founded Taschen Books, publisher of fine art books. As he noted, he saw no point in going to a university.

Channing Tatum, actor. Dropped out of Glenville State College at the age of 18 (after one semester). Became an actor after stints as a male dancer, construction worker, perfume spritzer and model.

Alfred Taubman, billionaire chairman of Sotheby, real estate investor, mall operator. Dropped out of the University of Michigan. Made his first fortune investing in shopping malls. Pledged a donation of $56 million to the University of Michigan in 2012.

Jack Crawford Taylor, billionaire founder of Enterprise Rent-a-Car. Dropped out of Washington University to serve as a fighter pilot in the Navy during World War II. Sold cars after the war before starting a car leasing company.

Noel Taylor, costume designer (stage and movies). Dropped out of school at the age of 16 to work in the theater, first as an actor.

Zachary Taylor, U.S. president, general. Little formal schooling. Home-schooled. Of the 44 people who served as president of the United States, 8 never went to college.

Timmy Teepell, chief of staff for Louisiana governor Bobby Jindal. A product of home schooling, he never attended college.

Justin Theroux, actor. Has joked about getting kicked out of school.

Kelly Thiebaud, model and actress. Her mother made her finish high school, but she never attended college. As she noted about staying in high school, "At the time I hated it. There's so much opportunity out there! But I'm thankful for it now, because the experience helped me stay grounded."

Danny Thomas, actor, producer, humanitarian. Dropped out of high school.

Dave Thomas, billionaire founder of Wendy's. As a youngster his family moved around a lot. While working as a busboy at the age of 15, he refused to move once again with the family. Instead, he dropped out of high school and went to work full time in a restaurant (moving in with the family that owned the restaurant).

Billy Bob Thornton, actor. After taking some classes at Henderson State University in Arkansas, he dropped out and headed for New York City to become a rock star. Four years later, he headed to Los Angeles to become an actor.

Uma Thurman, actress. Left boarding school at the age of 15 and moved to New York City to become an actress. Has not attended college.

Ashley Tisdale, singer and actress. Has not yet attended college.

Leo Tolstoy, count, novelist (*War and Peace, Anna Karenina*). Dropped out after three years at the university.

Marisa Tomei, Oscar-winning actress. Transferred from Boston University after one year to attend New York University, but dropped out within a year to continue her career as an actress.

Adam and Matthew Toren, founders of YoungEntrepreneur.com. As they noted on their website,

Entrepreneurs at an early age, Matthew and I had already started six (toot toot) businesses by the time we graduated high school. We were both offered college scholarships, but turned them down – it was clear to us that college was not in our future. Within a week of graduating high school, we bought a bar/café/billiards location, which we overhauled, re-branded and turned into a hot spot; and on the 12-month we sold it for a great profit.

Lynsi Torres, billionaire owner of In-N-Out Burger (inherited). Did not attend college.

Nick Tosches, novelist and biographer. Never attended college. As he noted in an interview in Esquire magazine: *"I wanted to just get a job so I could have enough money for my own apartment and be able to get drunk."*

Nina Totenberg, radio show host. Dropped out of Boston University.

Doris Eaton Travis, a Ziegfield Follies girl, actress, singer. Started at the Follies the day she finished eighth grade. Earned her high school diploma at the age of 77. Finally graduated from college at the age of 88.

John Travolta, actor. His parents allowed him to drop out of Dwight Morrow High School in Englewood, New Jersey for one year to pursue a theatrical career. He never returned.

Derek Trucks, singer and musician. Attended high school on the road while playing for the Allman Brothers Band. Never attended college.

Harry Truman, U.S. president. Never went to college.

Isaac Tshuva, billionaire builder, industrialist and hotelier. At the age of 12, he started working as a laborer to support his family while attending school at night. After three years in the Army, he skipped college to begin working in construction.

GATE KEY

Harriet Tubman, abolitionist, former slave, humanitarian, spy, nurse, suffragist. Did not attend college. A big promoter of education even though she was illiterate.

Frederick Tudor, the Ice King. Dropped out of school at the age of 13. After loafing for a few years, he retired to his family's country estate to fish, farm and hunt. Eventually, he began shipping ice from his Massachusetts pond to tropical countries for use in cooling drinks and making ice cream.

Ted Turner, billionaire founder of CNN and TBS, owner of Atlanta Braves, philanthropist, America's largest landowner with 1.8 million acres. Was asked to leave Brown University during his fourth year. Got suspended twice, once for having a girl in his room and he doesn't remember the second reason. "I'm down to a little more than a billion. You can get by on that if you really economize and don't buy a lot of planes and yachts and stuff."

Fred Tuttle, dairy farmer, actor. Dropped out of school in the 10th grade and spent most of his life as a farmer. Became a celebrity as a 77-year-old actor in the movie *Man with a Plan*.

Mark Twain (Samuel Langhorne Clemens), printer, riverboat pilot, prospector, newspaper reporter, humorist, bestselling novelist. Left school a year after his father's death, never went beyond the fifth grade. Nonetheless, he still wrote the first great American novel, *The Adventures of Huckleberry Finn*.

Jamie Tworkowski, surfer and founder of To Write Love on Her Arms. College drop-out. Also dropped out of high school, but eventually went back to finish. "It wasn't my choice to walk away from school. I was hanging around with guys older than me and I'd skip school to play with them. I kept missing more and more school, and I got busted for it finally. But I went back. I felt like I'd be a real stooge if I didn't at least finish high school."

Mike Tyson, heavyweight champion boxer, the first boxer to hold the WBA, WBC, and IBF heavyweight titles at the same time. Made his professional boxing debut at the age of 18. Never attended college.

Albert Ueltschi, billionaire founder of FlightSafety International pilot training schools. Dropped out of the University of Kentucky to follow his passion, flying planes. After flying for PanAm for ten years, he founded FlightSafety.

Donald Eugene Ulrich, aka Don Rich, country music guitarist and fiddler. Quit college to join The Buckaroos. The band had 19 #1 country hits during the 1960s.

Kate Upton, model, equestrian, actress, fashion designer. Has not attended college.

Leon Uris, bestselling novelist. Dropped out of high school at the age of 17 to join the U.S. Marines.

Dan Ushman, co-founder of SingleHop, a web hosting company. Dropped out of college during the first year to work on their first web hosting company, MidPhase.

Peter Ustinov, Oscar-winning actor. Dropped out of high school.

Buddy Valastro, baker and reality TV star (*Cake Boss*). Dropped out of high school to run the family baking business after his father died.

Jay Van Andel, billionaire co-founder of Amway (now Alticor). Served in the Army after high school. Founded Amway along with his best friend Richard DeVos.

Martin Van Buren, U.S. president. Little formal education. Began studying law at the age of 14 while apprenticing at a law firm. Of the 44 people who served as president of the United States, 8 never went to college.

Cornelius Vanderbilt, railroad magnate and one of the wealthiest Americans of the mid-1800s. Had little formal schooling. Was considered uncouth and illiterate until he became too rich to ignore.

Anton van Leeuwenhoek, microbiologist, microscope maker, discoverer of bacteria, blood cells and sperm cells. Dropped out of high school.

Jesse "The Body" Ventura, wrestler, actor, Minnesota governor. Dropped out of North Hennepin Community College after one year.

Lynn Vincent, bestselling ghost writer. Dropped out of college to join the Navy. Later left the military to write full-time. She had three books on the bestseller lists in the same week.

Kat Von D, aka Katherine Von Drachenberg, reality TV star, tattoo artist, skateboard designer, developer of makeup line. Dropped out of school at the age of 14.

Frank Vos, advertising executive, Frank Vos Agency. Did not finish college. But, when he retired, he sold his company and got a B.A. and M.A. in American history from Columbia University.

Andy Wachowski, screenwriter, director, *The Matrix*. Dropped out of Emerson College.

Donnie Wahlberg, Jr., singer (New Kids on the Block), actor, music producer. Never attended college. Started his singing career at the age of 15.

Mark Wahlberg, rapper (as Marky Mark), model, actor, producer, entrepreneur. Dropped out of school for the first time at the age of 13 and for good at the age of 16. Was in prison at the age of 16 for assault. Is currently working on his GED: "I will have that GED before my kids are old enough to know that Dad never did it."

Theodore Waitt, billionaire founder of Gateway Computers. Dropped out of the University of Iowa one semester short of a degree to start Gateway with his older brother in 1985.

Jimmy Wales, cofounder of Wikipedia. Attended grade school at a two-room school run by his mother and grandmother. Dropped out of a PhD program in economics at the University of Indiana to become a trader at Chicago Options Associates.

Alfred Russel Wallace, naturalist, co-discover of evolutionary theory. Left school at the age of 14 to go to work to support his family. Wallace was self-taught via frequent visits to libraries and workingman's institutes, while working as a land surveyor, a builder and a school teacher.

DeWitt Wallace, founder and publisher of *Reader's Digest*, philanthropist. Dropped out of Macalester College after one year. Dropped out of the University of California at Berkeley after the second year.

David Walsh, multimillionaire gambler, founder of the Museum of Old and New Art. Dropped out of college to make his fortune as a professional gambler (when he pooled his talent for mathematics with some friends to make money as a gambler).

Kate Walsh, actress. Dropped out of the University of Arizona at the age of 19 to pursue a career in acting.

Alexander Wang, fashion designer. Dropped out of Parsons The New School for Design after two years. As he noted, "I'm naive to the traditional design formula."

Y.C. Wang, billionaire founder of Formosa Plastics. Never attended high school.

Ty Warner, billionaire developer of Beanie Babies, hotel owner, real estate investor. He dropped out of Kalamazoo College to work as a busboy, valet parker, bellman and fruit vendor. Eventually he went on the road selling encyclopedias, cameras, and plush toys.

K'naan Warsame, aka K'naan the Skinny, Somali refugee, rapper and rock star. Dropped out of high school after the 10th grade. Was featured in a $300 million worldwide advertising campaign by Coca-Cola.

Dennis Washington, billionaire road contractor. The day after his high school graduation, he headed to Alaska to work in construction for two years. By the age of 22, he was working for his uncle on his first interstate highway job. He now owns a copper mine in Montana, a barge business in Vancouver and Montana Rail Link.

George Washington, U.S. president, general, plantation owner. Ended his education after a few years of elementary school. Of the 44 people who served as president of the United States, 8 never went to college.

Keith Waterhouse, journalist, comic novelist, *Billy Liar*. Was inspired to drop out of school and become a writer after reading Mark Twain and P.G. Wodehouse.

Naomi Watts, actress. Quit high school at the age of 17. "I told my mum I'm done with my education."

GATE KEY

John Wayne, actor, attended the University of Southern California for two years on a football scholarship. He dropped out to work as a prop man and stuntman for movie studios.

Lil Wayne (Dwayne Carter), rapper. Never attended college.

Michael Weatherly, actor, *Dark Angel* and *NCIS*. Dropped out of American University at the age of 21 to pursue acting full time.

Sidney Weinberg, managing partner of Goldman Sachs, aka Mr. Wall Street. Dropped out of the seventh grade in Brooklyn.

Jerry Weintraub, movie and music producer. Joined the Air Force instead of going to college. Later studied acting at Manhattan's Neighborhood Playhouse.

H.G. Wells, science fiction author. Dropped out of high school to help support his family. Eventually completed high school and went on to college.

Daria Werbowy, model. Has not yet attended college. Became the new face of Prada at the age of 19.

Paul Wesley, aka Paul Wasilewski, actor. "I was going to high school in *Guiding Light*, but getting kicked out of school in real life." Attended Rutgers University for one semester before dropping out to act full time.

Kanye West, Platinum rapper, record producer, fashion designer. Attended the American Academy of Art in Chicago for one semester and then transferred to Chicago State University, but dropped out to focus on his music career.

Leslie Wexner, billionaire founder of Limited Brands. Dropped out of Ohio State law school. Started the Limited with a $5,000 loan from an aunt.

Dean White, billionaire hotelier and billboard magnate. Dropped out of the University of Nebraska to join the Merchant Marine Academy. Served during World War II. Then took over family business after the war and built it into a billboard and real estate empire.

Shawn White, multi-millionaire Olympic snowboarder and X-Games skateboarder. Did not attend college. Turned pro in skateboarding at the age of 16.

Walt Whitman, poet, self-publisher. Elementary school dropout.

Kristen Wiig, comedienne, actress. Took an acting class her freshman year at the University of Arizona, got the acting bug, dropped out after one year and headed to Los Angeles to make it as an actress. But according to an interview in *Marie Claire*, Kristen went to college in Virginia and dropped out after a year, headed to Mexico for three months of vagabonding and then worked in Arizona before heading to Los Angeles.

GATE KEY

Dan Wilks, billionaire founder of Wilks Masonry and Frak Tech. Did not attend college.

Farris Wilks, billionaire founder of Wilks Masonry and Frak Tech. Did not attend college.

Olivia Wilde, actress. Instead of going to Bard College after graduating from Andover Prep, she left for Hollywood to become an actress. Has not yet attended college.

Evan Williams, billionaire co-developer of Blogger, Twitter, and Medium social blogging platform. He dropped out of the University of Nebraska to write computer code.

Michelle Williams, actress. Was legally emancipated at the age of 15 from her family. Never went to college.

Vanessa Williams, actress, singer, model, Miss America. She received a scholarship and attended Syracuse University as a Musical Theatre Arts major. She left during her sophomore year to fulfill her duties as Miss America and subsequently left the university to focus on her entertainment career. Twenty-five years later, she graduated from Syracuse by earning her remaining college credits through her life experience.

Marianne Williamson, spiritual author, politician. Attended college in Pomona, California for two years before dropping out.

Bruce Willis, actor. Dropped out of the theater program of Montclair State University after his junior year. He asserts that a college diploma "is just a trophy. I have some bowling trophies I think would be worth about the same thing."

Gretchen Wilson, country singer. Quit school after the eighth grade. Finally earned her GED equivalency degree in 2009.

I've wanted to go back and get my GED for years, ever since I quit school after the eighth grade. I had a troubled childhood and I just wanted to get out of the house and on with life as quickly as possible. And back then I thought it wasn't important to have a high school diploma to chase my music dreams. But I always knew that finishing high school would make me feel a little more complete. (*Redbook* Magazine)

Kemmons Wilson, multimillionaire founder of Holiday Inns. Dropped out of high school.

Owen Wilson, actor, screenwriter. Dropped out of the University of Texas.

Anna Wintour, editor-in-chief, *Vogue* Magazine. Did not attend college.

Reese Witherspoon, Oscar-winning actress and model. Starred in her first film at the age of 14. Enrolled in Stanford University, but dropped out to pursue acting full time.

Lee Ann Womack, country music singer. She attended South Plains Junior College for one year and then took a few classes at Belmont University, but she never graduated.

"I interned at MCA Records and learned more from that internship than I ever did in the classroom." — Lee Ann Womack (*Woman's Day* Magazine)

Tyrone Wood, director of Scream Gallery, son of Rolling Stone's Ronnie Wood. Education: "The school of life."

Shailene Woodley, actress. Has not yet attended college, but "I definitely want to go to college, but right now I'm taking my life lessons backpacking and gardening and learning how to make tables."

Tiger Woods, multimillionaire golfer, at one point the best golfer in the world. He turned pro at the age of 20 after attending Stanford University for a year or two.

Steve Wozniak, billionaire co-founder of Apple. Dropped out of college.

Frank Lloyd Wright, architect, interior designer, leader of the Prairie School of Architecture. Voted as the greatest American architect of all time by the American Institute of Architects. Attended a high school in Madison, Wisconsin, but apparently never graduated. He was admitted to the University of Wisconsin as a special student and took classes part-time for two semesters. He left school at the age of 20 to work at an architectural firm in Chicago, Illinois.

Orville Wright, inventor of the airplane. Dropped out of high school in his junior year to open a printing business.

Wilbur Wright, inventor of the airplane. Completed four years of high school, but never received his diploma. Did not attend college.

William Wrigley, Jr., founder of Wrigley's chewing gum. Also owner of the Chicago Cubs, Wrigley Field, Arizona Biltmore Hotel and Catalina Island. Expelled from grammar school. Never attended high school or college.

Jason Wu, fashion designer. After high school, he studied at Parsons New School for Design, but left before graduating to intern with a designer.

Hiroshi Yamauchi, multi-millionaire CEO of Nintendo. Dropped out of college.

Jerry Yang, billionaire co-founder of Yahoo! Dropped out of the Stanford University PhD program to create Yahoo!

Adam Yauch, aka MCA of the Beastie Boys, rapper, songwriter, film director, Buddhist. He attended Bard College for two years before dropping out.

Anton Yelchin, actor. "I was going to go to USC and study political theory, but I really love movies.

They're pretty much my favorite things, so I figured I would just keep doing this."

Chaleo Yoovidhya, billionaire. Little formal education, but he still founded a pharma business in the 1960s that developed eventually into the Red Bull energy drink business.

Jay-Z (Shawn Carter), rapper, entrepreneur, owner of Rocawear clothing, co-owner of Brooklyn Nets basketball team. Never attended college. "I'm a thinker. I figure things out. I don't have a high level of education, but I'm practical--and I have great instincts."

Babe Didrikson Zaharias, golfer, basketball player, Olympic track and field star. Did not attend college.

Frank Zappa, rock musician. Probably dropped out of college. As he noted in liner notes for his *Freak Out* album, "Drop out of school before your mind rots from our mediocre educational system."

Catherine Zeta-Jones, actress. Dropped out of school at the age of 15 to join a touring production of *The Pajama Game*.

Mark Zuckerberg, billionaire founder of Facebook. Dropped out of Harvard to continue working on the social networking website he founded in his dorm room in 2004. Facebook has more than 300 million users.
- *The above names appear courtesy of College Drop outs Hall of Fame.*

Insurance Professional

Gate Keys

1. Image
2. Character
3. Hard Work and Determination
4. Qualifications and Certifications
5. Good Credit
6. No Criminal Record
7. Clean Driving Record

Estimated Salary: $30,000 - $150,000 a year

Certifications: Property & Casualty, Life and Health and or Series 6 63 license.

Required age to start: 18

The insurance business is a Billion dollar industry that's really recession proof. Anyone that owns a home or car is required by their State to have insurance coverage on that home and or vehicle. Most Apartments and or Landlords also require that their tenants have Renters Insurance. Insurance protects you, your Family and others. Depending on your license you may work in several fields of insurance, all which garner a healthy salary. By applying the 7 gate keys within this profession one can guarantee a Great Quality of Life. Some examples of the different types of insurance are described on the following pages.

GATE KEY

Selling P&C: Your Property and Casualty license allows you to work in the most common fields of insurance also known as Home and Auto. With your P&C license you can sell Home Owners Insurance, Renters Insurance, Business Insurance, Auto Insurance, Motorcycle Insurance, Malpractice Insurance, Commercial Insurance and more within the P&C line.

Adjuster: If sales are not your field, you can choose to work as an Adjuster. This is when you go out to look at the damage that was done to the property. As an Adjuster, it will be your duty to calculate the amount of money needed to bring the customers property back to its full state. If the property can be repaired, you will have the authority to write them a check for that amount on the spot if not sending it by mail.

Underwriting: Another option you have with your P&C line is to work in the Underwriting department. In Underwriting you are responsible for pre-qualifying a customer for insurance based on their risk assessment. For example, if you have two college students in a fraternity renting an apartment and they applied for Renters Insurance versus two teenagers who work 9-6 every day, which two will likely incur the most risk? It would be the college students because they will more than likely have parties and more visitors which put them, their friends and the apartment at more risk than the working teens.

Claims: Now, if Sales, Adjusting and Underwriting are not of any interest to you then you can always work in claims. This is when the customers call in to initiate a claim because of an incident that they caused or in which they were involved. This is why everyone buys insurance. Customers will depend on you to make sure that their claim is filed and will pay as promised. On the other hand, all claims are not paid, some claims just don't meet the criteria and as a Claim Specialist it will be your duty to inform the customer of this as well.

Life & Health Insurance: Having a Life and Health License will allow you to sell Life Insurance and perform the same duties just as stated above with a P&C license, but in the Life & Health sector.

The Series 6 63 allows you to sell Life Insurance Annuities and Mutual Funds in addition to Life Insurance. As an Insurance Professional you may elect to become licensed in all of the above fields to maximize your income and Professional Pedigree. To acquire your Insurance License you must take the Pre-Licensing course which is usually 40 hours or a week long course. Once you have received a completion certificate for that class, you must then take the State Insurance License exam and pass it to receive your license. There is a fee for the pre-licensing class, the books, the test and your license. Please check with your States Insurance Department for all needed information to become licensed.

GATE KEY

Firefighter

Gate Keys

1. Image
2. Character
3. Hard Work and Determination
4. Qualifications and Certifications
5. Good Credit
6. No Criminal Record
7. Clean Driving Record

Estimated Salary: $43,000 - $83,990 a year

Certifications: Firefighters Exam, Physical, Diploma, Must pass drug test and background check.

Required age to start: 21 and 35 is the cut off age.

    Being a Firefighter is one of the most Honored Professions that one can have. The job itself is dangerous, but we the people depend on this profession every day to help protect us from danger and rescue us in the unlikely event of a fire and many other hazardous situations. To become a firefighter you must pass a written and physical exam. The starting age is 21, but if you are serious about becoming a Professional Firefighter you may want to start by getting a job at your local fire department or helping out around the station until you become of age.

A person can make a good living as a firefighter and by applying the 7 gate keys at an early age you can mold yourself into a great professional. To date the State of California pays the most for this profession. It's very important to take in account the risk you will take as a firefighter. One must be in very good shape because of the everyday challenges you will face. The cut off age to apply is 35 and you may have some leeway due to your physical condition, if you are prior military. One should contact their local Safety and Fire Commission to make sure they are taking all the necessary steps to become a Firefighter.

GATE KEY

Truck Driver

Gate Keys

1. **Image**
2. **Character**
3. **Hard Work and Determination**
4. **Qualifications and Certifications**
5. Good Credit
6. No Criminal Record
7. **Clean Driving Record**

Estimated Salary: $30,000 - $100,990 a year

Certifications: Commercial Driver License; Truck Driving School.

Required age to start: 18

The duty of a truck driver is to transport cargo to and from a specific destination. Your truck usually weighs more than 3 tons. It is the responsibility of the driver to make sure that your cargo is at the drop off point on time according to your manifest. All truck drivers are required to attend truck driving school to obtain a CDL for the job. Salaries differ depending on your job and route and even the type of cargo you carry. For example, a driver transporting gasoline or hazardous material will make more than someone transporting a trailer full of cereal.

As a driver you will work closely with your dispatcher because that will be the person in charge of your routes and keeping track of your schedule. You will also have to abide by Government and State laws when it comes to cargo, weight, etc. Keeping a log of your daily routine is mandatory and most times this log is also used to track how you get paid.

It should also be noted that the life of a truck driver is for someone that likes driving and being on the road. You will travel to many places and meet all kinds of people. For some it's an adventure and for others it's a job. The one thing it will do is put food on your table and make for a good living. Just be prepared to do plenty of traveling.

Truck Driving School is usually between 3 and 7 weeks long depending on the school you choose. The cost of school can be $2500 - $6500, which isn't a bad investment, considering the money you are going to make with your license. If you choose to work for a company that sponsors a school, admission could be less. You can acquire your CDL at 18, but you will probably have some limits when it comes to driving intrastate. Truck driving schools can be found all across the U.S.A and Canada; do your research and find the school that works best for you.

GATE KEY

Real Estate Agent

Gate Keys

1. **Image**
2. **Character**
3. **Hard Work and Determination**
4. **Qualifications and Certifications**
5. Good Credit
6. **No Criminal Record**
7. Clean Driving Record

Estimated Salary: $38,000 - $100,000 a year

Certifications: Real Estate License

Required age to start: 18

Real Estate Agents can provide hundreds of different, creative options for a person to purchase a home, land or business and commercial property. The buyer truly benefits because Real Estate Agents are not employees of any particular company or financial institution, but instead have a working relationship with a broad range of companies that serve the public by helping them buy or sell real estate.

To become a Real Estate Agent you must attend a 60-hour pre-licensing course and successfully pass your States Real Estate exam after the class. You can take the class once you're 18 years of age. I would recommend you intern in a Real Estate office once you reach legal working age to familiarize yourself with the business. Learn the lingo, shadow some agents and experience what your future will look like. The Real Estate market however is a fickle one and rules and laws are very strict, so pay close attention and take your profession very seriously.

You should contact your States Real Estate commission for any questions regarding testing or what necessary steps you may need to take. Every State can vary. Out of the 7 Gate Keys, Image, Character and Hard Work along with Determination are the best ones to sharpen at an early age when entering this field. Build on the other 4 as you mature, they should become apparent while you mold yourself into a Real Estate Professional.

GATE KEY

Armed Forces

Gate Keys

1. Image
2. Character
3. Hard Work and Determination
4. Qualifications and Certifications
5. Good Credit
6. No Criminal Record
7. Clean Driving Record

Estimated Salary: $16,000 - $150,000 a year

Certifications: ASVAB, Multiple-Aptitude Battery Test

Required age to start: 18

As a proud Veteran, I'm going to tell you that if you want to get paid in the military and make it a profession, setting your goal on being an Officer is the way to go. You must first look at the risk versus the job and if it equates to the pay you desire. The Armed Forces in many ways is like corporate America when it comes to pay and its positions. But, having the knowledge and an early start will put you ahead of the game and on the right track. If you look at the pay scale detailed above on the 'Estimated Salary' line, it's obvious that someone is way at the bottom of the scale. One of the benefits of this book? If you pay close attention, I will tell you how to come out on top, but you must put in the work!

Soldiers, Marines, Seaman and Airman all have enlisted pay grades which start with E1. If you are in ROTC then you should have an idea of what rank means in these fields. If you're not in ROTC and you're considering the Military as a profession, you should enroll in ROTC before you leave High School. ROTC will help you acclimate to the military way of life and will count as credit towards your rank when entering the Armed Forces. Now, if you are interested in earning a six figure income while fighting for your Country, you must thrive to be an Officer. The Privates, Corporals, Specialists, Sergeants, Staff Sergeants, Master Sergeants, etc. will not award you this income.

To make the big bucks, you must first show that you know how to lead by coming up through the ranks and making it as a Non Commissioned Officer, ie. Sergeant! Once you become a NCO you may apply to The Army's OCS aka Officer Candidates School. The rigorous course is usually 12 weeks long and for those who complete it successfully you will receive formal commissions as a U.S Army Officer and assume the ability to command Soldiers. The Marines, Navy and Air Force all have an Officer Candidates School as well. All of them, however, are designed to give you the framework to perform your duties as a unit commander. Amongst other things, you will learn tactics training, how to deal with mental and emotional stress and how to give orders.

To achieve this you must work hard, stay focused and be determined to succeed. It will not be easy, but

GATE KEY

the reward is worth every rigorous second you devote to your goal. You must be between 19 and 28 years old to apply for Officers School and eligible for a secret security clearance. All 7 Gate Keys should be applied to obtain this profession. To join any branch of the Armed Forces, you should visit a recruiter in your area.

Night Club Owner

Gate Keys

1. Image
2. Character
3. Hard Work and Determination
4. Qualifications and Certifications
5. Good Credit
6. No Criminal Record
7. Clean Driving Record

Estimated Salary: $80,000 - $2,000,000 a year

Certifications: Business License, Corporation, Alcohol License, Resale License, Tax I.D Number

Required age to start: 18

This profession has several moving parts each that you must learn and build along your journey to opening a Night Club. The knowledge you are about to receive will put you years ahead of the game, if you follow the steps. All of your Gate Keys are important in this profession, without them you will not succeed. As a teenager you will not be able to open a club that sells alcohol, so your focus should be a teen club which is a good way to start your profession; then when you turn 21 you can increase revenue by opening a second club for the older crowd or transform your teen club into one for the 21 and older crowd. If you're serious about your money and this profession, you will keep both of them open. Here are some important steps to help you get started.

High School: During school you should start promoting parties among your peers. This is where your following or fan base begins. The beautiful thing about a dream is that it starts as an idea. Take this idea and make it a reality. While in school you can throw parties celebrating a fellow student's birthday, college signings, after game parties; be creative. If you can't use the school for this event, find a teenage-friendly venue and always charge a small door fee. Some venues may want to charge a rental fee, but if you have any kind of business savvy about you, you can negotiate that fee to work with your budget and make it work. Remember, this is your dream and you make the rules.

Street Team: A street team is the oil that will make your dream run. The team should consist of friends or people that you assemble to help get the news out about your events. Their main job will be to distribute fliers, pin up posters and spread the word physically in the street and among your peers. You should always be creative when using your street team, when the people see them they will see you. So, make sure that your message is clear and choose your promoting territory wisely; do not equate social media to a physical street team, people will want to feel and see your energy, too.

Door Man: Outside of yourself, this will be the most important person in your operation. This must be someone that you can trust and he or she should not bend or waiver for anyone. Their main and only job will be to get your door fee and to check Id's. If there is to be a VIP list, he or she will be the only one that has it and all money and VIP's will go through him or her. This way you have one person responsible for reporting earnings for the event and he or she will act as a shield between you and those that will be trying to get in free or asking for special treatment.

It's important to remember that you as the owner or CEO should not be at the door taking money, you will lose money just by being there because as the star of the show you will try to appease your patrons and let some people in free because if you don't, you just may well lose them. Simply don't put yourself in that position. Always have a set time to open and make sure you have specials in place for the ladies. Guys come to see girls and you will need them there to keep the party going. Your doorman must remain at the door until the end of the event. If you see where you can charge more for a VIP entrance, do it!

DJ: The DJ will be the engine to your machine. Do not choose your DJ according to friendship, but on skill set and ability to keep the crowd hype. A lame DJ will make your night a nightmare! Select several DJ's to use for your events. If they're worth their salt, each of them will have a fan base that will follow them as well. This is why it's important to keep your DJ selection diverse, their fans become yours and vice versa.

Social Network Promoter: In today's world you will need an individual or team of people that are solely responsible for promoting your club and/or events via social media. With the current flow of Facebook, Twitter, Instagram, etc. it's easy to post your events to thousands or even millions in seconds. This team should promote and build your following on a daily basis. Once the event takes place, it's important for them to be there promoting the event as well as to capture pictures and videos to post live and to add to your stock footage. Remember people want to be seen! This will also make them interact during the event via social media, causing self-promotion.

Graphic Designer: The graphic designer is the one person that can create a visual for your club or event. It is very important that you find a great GD because you want your visual to be spectacular. Your fliers, posters and any image that you want created should come through this person before it hits the streets. Always make sure the graphic designer creates a file for web promotion and one for print. The images are formatted differently and are not interchangeable. You will want to promote the same flier via social media that you have on the street.

Security: Security will be responsible for protecting your investment, your dream, your baby--I'm sure you get the idea! He also will be in charge of keeping the patrons safe. If you want a long successful career as a club owner, make sure that your security doesn't take any non-sense. No weapons or drugs should be allowed in your event and no alcohol while operating a teen club. Your security staff should be staffed according to size of event or the amount of people that you are expecting. One of your security guys should be at the door with a ticker, taking head count while the other is searching patrons. More should be patrolling inside.

Always mix it up when you choose a security guard to take head count. You will need the head count at the end of the night to equate your money to the number of people that attended. I always made the patrons sign in as well, that way I had door count three times: one count from the Doorman by the amount of money, the sign in sheet and the ticker. When selecting your security staff, remember that you want to keep people safe not crush their skulls! Some guards will go on the defense before rectifying the problem and escorting the patron out. When this happens you will start losing your fan base faster than you can blink an eye. Trust me you don't want to be that guy known for having patrons beat up.

Strong Team: Your team should consist of Doorman, Street Team, DJ, Social Network Promoter & Marketer, Graphic Designer and Security. With these people in place you can start planning your first night.

Building Brand: You will experience many obstacles and Nay Sayers, but remember to stay focused! Keep to the plan and make your team strong. You must constantly feed them your dream in which they decided to take part. You only get one first impression, make it count and you all will prosper. It's important for you to know what you want your brand to look like in order to build it.

Network: Remember that you are the boss and you make your own rules. While in the beginning stages to your Club Owner profession, practice cross promoting with like-minded individuals within your school or other schools, if you like. Try doing some events together and using each other's' resources. You could also get involved in community events by helping the organizations with an event or sponsoring it, like car washes, food fundraisers, etc. All of this will help build your brand.

"Your Net Worth is only as big as your Network!"

- Rev. Run

Following: This will be the patrons that you picked up along the way. The people you impress will be the same people that will make you your first million. The devotion one person can provide to your success along the way speaks volumes. Cherish every one of them and treat them how you would want to be treated. Every word, every action and every second that you devote to this profession depends on it.

Location: When choosing a location for your club, make sure that the city's population can support your dream. Ask questions like:

- *Is there any competition?*
- *Can this economy afford what I have to offer?*
- *How much does the average person in the area earn?*
- *What is the population of teenagers or 21 and over adults in the area? How much is rent?*
- *What can I afford to pay each month?*

Questions like these will prevent headaches down the road and stop you from making a bad decision.

If you're opening a teen club in the area that your school's in, be sure to pick a location that all of your patrons can get to easily. Running a teen nightclub on the weekends and going to High School during the week can be done!

Lease: This is one of the most important steps in opening your club. You will have to decide on what your budget will be. Depending on where you live, you can get a decent sized building for a good amount. If you're in a small town, you can get them dirt cheap. If you're in a larger city, then you're going to pay more of course!

My very first club was only $350 a month. I didn't sell alcohol and all my money came from the door. I made $1500 to $3200 a week and my overhead was only $350 plus a phone bill that averaged $129 a month. Take it from me kids, there's money to be made in a teen club. I saved that money then opened a larger club a year later for the 21 and over crowd with a bar.

GATE KEY

When searching for a location be patient and do your research before deciding. If you're under 18, you may have to get a parent, friend or relative to sign the lease for you. No worries; just make them a silent partner and you guys work out the specifics of how they can profit by helping you. That relationship alone can garner much fruit in the future. You will need a down payment to start the lease. It's usually 1st month's rent plus a deposit. The deposit depends on the landlord. If you're lucky enough to start your club profession journey early, you should have your own funds to pay the down payment by the time you reach this stage.

Liquor License: Liquor is the gas that will keep your dream moving, once you turn 21 and take it to the next level. This is when you will need to apply for a liquor license with your state. I cannot stress how important it is that you apply all of the Gate Keys during your journey before this process. Once you apply, the licensing board will post a letter in the local newspaper and on your club door for all to see. The letter is to notify anyone in the area and county that you are applying for a liquor license at your club.

The community or any one person will have 30-45 days depending on the state to file a complaint against you getting a license at your club. If there is anyone that you pissed off, kicked out of a party or just weren't nice to when they came to your event, trust me, that person will be in the back of your mind as you wait those 30-45 days in hoping that they don't file a complaint against your liquor license process.

(Now you see why building a good brand is important.) Some felonies, back child support and any DUI can prevent you from getting your liquor license. (Each state varies.)

Once the waiting period is over and you have no complaints, you will be able to sell alcohol. Liquor is sold in shots and there are 20-22 shots in a bottle according to the bottle that clubs are allowed to use. Most states use liter bottles. That bottle wholesales to you for $18-$32. Now, pay close attention and do your math! If you sell 22 shots at $8 a shot and the bottle cost $20, how much profit is that?--$156.00 per bottle! Yep! Welcome to the Night Club Industry!

Business License: This is needed to conduct business in your city or county. This can be obtained from your County Clerk's Office. Also inquire about a LLC, Limited Partnership, C Corporation or S Corp.

Resale License: Needed to sell goods in your city or county. This can also be obtained from your County Clerk's office as well.

Tax I.D Number: Needed to pay taxes for business. It can be obtained from the IRS.

Protect and apply all 7 Gate Keys, if you want to succeed!

GATE KEY

Auto Detail Shop

Gate Keys

1. Image
2. Character
3. Hard Work and Determination
4. Qualifications and Certifications
5. Good Credit
6. No Criminal Record
7. Clean Driving Record

Estimated Salary: $50,000 - $200,000 a year

Certifications: Business License, Corporation, Tax ID Number

Required age to start: 16

The Auto Detail Business or as it is most commonly known, "the Car Wash Business" can be a very lucrative one. Let's just look at some simple logistics. Say for example, you wash 30 cars a day for four days a week. That's 120 cars and you charge $20 for each car. That's $3,200 a week. This number can be smaller or larger depending on the set up of your operation. For this profession, the organization of your business will play a huge part in the money you make.

To be successful you will want to maximize your value. Make sure you have a great location, whether stationary or mobile, and a hard working staff. Next, you will want to build price points for the services that you will be offering so that you can see profit. You will not only be washing cars, but building relationships with patrons and potential business clients as well. You must earn their trust and make them happy with your great service! You want to eventually build a steady client base where you see your customers regularly and those that they will be referring to you as well. I've listed some important points below to help you get started.

Job Description: To wash, wax, vacuum, shampoo and polish vehicles while providing excellent customer service to your patrons. Attracting repeat business should be your goal.

Cashier: Should be someone that you can trust and must be dependable. You will count on this person to collect all monies due while patrons wait on their vehicles or pick them up.

Tips: Patrons will tip your employees depending on the job they have done and the overall customer service experience.

Wash and Rinse: For a large operation, I would recommend assigning employees to a certain position. A smaller operation can combine the duties, but of course will make less money because of the amount of vehicles you can service at one time. With that being said, you can have a team that wash and rinse only depending on your size and volume.

GATE KEY

Dryer: Make sure that you have the right materials when it comes to drying off vehicles. You don't want to leave streaks or lint on your customer's car.

Tires: This person will be responsible for cleaning the rims and oiling the tires.

Inside car: Should be a team of two people, one to vacuum and the other oiling the dash, doors and seats, etc.

Windows: Should consist of two people cleaning the inside and outside of the windows.

Shampoo: This should be an optional service that you offer having one person dedicated to shampoo at a designated area on the lot.

Wax: This is another optional service that you should offer having one or two people assigned to wax at a designated area on the lot.

Location: This will be a very important part to your business. You should find a location that's easy to get to and near a busy street or highway. Please make sure that you have enough water spouts on the building to service your needs as well as a good city or county drainage system. Your most costly overhead will be your water bill! The building can be inexpensive and you can pay your employees minimum wage because their tips will supplement their low income. (These steps are also important if you choose to go mobile and rent a location on the weekend.) You may also rent or purchase a water drum with a pressure pump to detail cars from a mobile set up or provide an on-call service.

License: You will need a business license, corporation and resale license which all can be obtained at your local County-Clerk's Office. Your Tax ID number may be obtained from the IRS.

Here's an example of what your price board should resemble:

1. Basic Wash (Wash & Rinse only) $15
2. Basic Plus Vacuum $20
3. Basic, Vacuum and Armor Oil Inside. $25
4. Basic, Vacuum & Armor Oil Inside & Out $30
5. Deluxe (All of the above plus Shampoo) $60
6. Super Deluxe (Deluxe, Shampoo & Wax) $110
7. Wax Only $65
8. Shampoo Only $40

GATE KEY

Painter

Gate Keys

1. **Image**
2. **Character**
3. **Hard Work and Determination**
4. **Qualifications and Certifications**
5. Good Credit
6. No Criminal Record
7. Clean Driving Record

Estimated Salary: $30,000 - $200,000 a year

Certifications: Business License, Corporation, Tax ID Number, Business Owners Insurance

Required age to start: 16

The profession of a painter is one that doesn't garner much attention, but is very necessary. Every building, home, church, school etc. at one point needs to be painted. No school is required to be a professional painter, only on the job experience. A gainfully employed painter can make $30 to $50 an hour. That's pretty good pay, but why not own your own painting company and make more? Here are a few steps that you can take to get started.

Experience: Find a company that you can work a few jobs with just to get the swing of things. Learn all you can about technique, mixing, equipment and even where to buy the paint for the best prices. Ask any questions that may come to mind.

Negotiator: If you don't possess the skills to negotiate a deal, then find someone that does and put them on your team. This person is very vital to your success and they will be responsible for landing you lucrative contracts by seeking out small and large job opportunities.

Employees: It doesn't take much skill to be a painter, just hard work and dedication. Hire a few people on your staff that have experience. The more painters that you have at your disposal the better it will be. This is important because the size of the contracts that your negotiator can get depends on your company's ability to deliver quality and meet deadlines.

Contracts: Your negotiator should contact construction companies, apartment complexes, home owners, government agencies, schools, hospitals and more to put in bids for upcoming jobs. These contracts can range in the thousands, sometimes millions. So, don't place a bid that you can't fulfill.

Business Owners Insurance: Before any company gives you a contract you must have Business Owners Insurance or General Liability Insurance to cover their interest and your company's as well. This insurance assures the company that's hiring you that they won't be liable for any accidents caused by you and your staff. If their company is at fault, don't worry they will have insurance to cover that incident as well. If you're not sure about them having insurance, be sure to ask.

Targets: I say go after the big fish like government projects, apartment complexes, gyms, schools, colleges, etc.

License: You will need your business license and Tax ID number. A business license may be obtained from County Clerk's office and a Tax ID from the IRS. For Business Owners Insurance, find a local insurance agent to help you with the process.

Landscaping

Gate Keys

1. Image
2. Character
3. Hard Work and Determination
4. Qualifications and Certifications
5. Good Credit
6. No Criminal Record
7. Clean Driving Record

Estimated Salary: $30,000 - $200,000 a year

Certifications: Business License, Corporation, Tax ID Number, Business Owners Insurance

Required age to start: 13

As a little boy I remember helping my Grandmother plant tulips. She showed me how deep to dig the hole and how to place the tulip bulb inside just right so that it would sprout up in the right direction. We would choose different colors, yellow, purple or red. As the weeks passed I monitored them everyday checking their progress. My Grandmother loved to landscape her yard. The grass stayed cut and the hedges groomed. Hell, I probably tore up at least three lawn mowers over the summers mowing her lawn, my mom's, aunt's and my great Grandmother's too! This had come to be a weekly Saturday thing and no, I didn't like it! But, I loved seeing the yards after they were mowed and groomed.

The best thing about all of that landscaping was that the neighbors wanted me to do theirs, too. So, I did, but not for free! Every summer I made extra cash to buy my school clothes just from what my Grandmother taught me about keeping her yard groomed. As far as a career in landscaping, it wasn't for me, but for those of you that enjoy it, there's plenty of money to be made! If you're in the position to start early while in high school, take advantage of the situation and start building your business now. The experience will be priceless. I've listed some great things to consider when starting your landscaping business.

Duties: Mow the lawn, trim hedges, rake leaves, snow removal, anything that you can do to beautify the landscape for your client. Your duties will also depend on your environment as well as climate.

Experience: The fastest way to become experienced in this profession would be to find work for a summer or two with a local landscaping company before you start your own. This will get you familiar with other techniques such as aeration, installing sprinkler systems, planting trees, flowers, shrubbery, etc.

Equipment: You will need the right equipment to start making good money as a landscaper. Lawn mowers, weed eaters, rakes, shovels, leaf blowers, etc.

The right equipment will equate to the better paying jobs and more contracts.

Staff: Landscaping is a labor job, but having the right people performing the right duties is still very important even though most anyone can perform general labor jobs. I would make sure that everyone has a specific duty. Place the right employee in the position that fits them and make sure their good at it.

Income: You should set prices for every job. Have a certain price for mowing. (This should vary with the size of the lawn as should most of your price points.) Charge for: Raking, Trimming, Aeration, Planting, Installing Sprinkler Systems, Lawn Lighting, etc.

License: All of your licensing can be obtained at your local County Clerk's office except for your Tax ID number which can be obtained from the IRS. For Business Owners Insurance, find a local insurance agent to help you with the process.

Comedian

Gate Keys

1. **Image**
2. **Character**
3. **Hard Work and Determination**
4. **Qualifications and Certifications**
5. Good Credit
6. No Criminal Record
7. Clean Driving Record

Estimated Salary: $10,000 - $200,000,000 a year

Certifications: The Natural ability to make people laugh.

Required age to start: 13

The comedic profession is one that requires a lot of hard work, focus, determination, tough skin and stage presence. Some people are just naturally gifted when it comes to making people laugh. Laughter is good for the soul; everyone needs a good laugh every now and then. Many greats, such as: Red Foxx, Richard Pryor, George Burns, Bill Cosby, Jim Carey, Eddie Murphy, Rosie O'Donnell, Jamie Foxx, Whoopi Goldberg, Chris Rock, Steve Harvey, Martin Lawrence, Kevin Hart, Bernie Mac and Carroll Burnett to name a few have made millions just from making people laugh.

I would say that Gate Keys, 1-3 are the most important when you start your journey down this path. Success doesn't come over night, you will have to hear the "boos", play the empty clubs, perform for free or for less than nothing and God only knows what else. The most important thing to intake while going through this process is to hone your craft, find your niche, what works for you.

Image: As a comedian think about how you want people to perceive you. Do you want them to laugh when they see you? Will a costume be a part of your act? Do you want to take the Steve Harvey approach, suit and tie? Eddie Murphy made his mark by being raw and uncut while appealing as a sex symbol to the ladies when he hit the stage. But, on the same token he played some funny characters as well as serious ones on television and in movies.

This is why it's important to practice, practice, practice, until you perfect your craft. Find out what people like about your comedy act the most and build on it. Jamie Foxx, Red Foxx and Whoopi Goldberg came up with stage names for their acts and became those people. They built an image! Just take a second and think about some of the comedians I've named and see what comes to mind when you think of them. That's the image they built!

Hard work: High School is a perfect place to start your comedic career. Where else will your fans be most honest? Start performing in your school talent shows. Play the dozens with your friends, telling momma jokes to each other. This is the battle ground when it comes to jokes.

Depending on what city you are in, you should sign up at the local comedy spots around town. Start building your image, go watch a few shows a week even if you have to sneak in. You don't become successful by not taking chances, so as soon as the opportunity comes for you to get on that stage, take it! Keep taking it, over and over again until you become great at it. Good isn't good enough, you have to aim to be GREAT! If you want the millions that your predecessors are making, then you will have to get off your butt and get to work!

Character: This is how you will be measured in the face of defeat as well as success. If you have a bad night and no one laughs at your jokes, will you quit or go write more? When a veteran in the business offers you some sound advice, will you listen or shrug it off? Even if your peers hate on you, you should still remain professional and stay focused on your goal! The sky is the limit when it comes to this profession, you make the rules.

The Jump: The time will come when you feel that you have perfected your craft. Everyone laughs at your jokes while you're in school cracking on anyone that looks like a victim to you. The local spots are showing you support and you're feeling like a star, but there's no money! Well, this is when you take that jump! If you're not in California, New York or Atlanta! Get to one of those cities in a hurry no matter what it takes and no matter who you have to leave behind. Success is about taking chances and sacrifice is the price we pay for it!

Whatever city you choose, be sure to continue your routine by frequenting the local comedy spots and events. Get your name and face out there! If I were you, I would go from NYC to California to Atlanta every other month! Hit every comedy spot, go to several casting calls and read for Movie and TV Roles. This is it, you're on ground zero and you shouldn't let anything or anyone stand in your way. This routine will help you build a name in the industry, so don't mess it up. Find a way to make it happen.

Bail Bondsman

Gate Keys

1. **Image**
2. **Character**
3. **Hard Work and Determination**
4. **Qualifications and Certifications**
5. Good Credit
6. **No Criminal Record**
7. Clean Driving Record

Estimated Salary: $20,000 - $200,000 a year

Certifications: Business License, Corporation, Tax ID Number, Bail Bondsman and Bounty Hunters Training, Bondsman Pre-Licensing Class and Surety Bondsman License.

Required age to start: 18 (states vary)

The Bail Bondsman or Bondswoman profession is a 700 Million dollar a year business. It takes a certain individual to take on this profession. You must be willing to put your life on the line. You will be working with jails, prisons, attorney's and law enforcement every day. As a Bondsman you will post bail, capture targets and collect money from people in whom you will have a financial interest. An insurance underwriter will be writing the bond for your clients, which means the profession is closely regulated by the insurance industry.

In some cases your clients will jump bail and it will be up to you to apprehend them in order to recoup your financial interest. Most individuals in this profession desire the need for a high adrenaline rush. If you like being in dangerous and compromising situations, this profession will not disappoint!

License: Contact your States Department of Insurance for info on pre-licensing class and Bondsman License. Business License can be obtained from the County Clerk's Office. Tax ID can be obtained from the IRS.

Training: Locate a Bounty Hunter and Bondsman training school in your area.

Skill Set: Requires a highly motivated and driven individual. I would suggest working for a Bondsman while in High School to get your feet wet, make sure this is the profession you want to pursue. It can be very financially rewarding, but also very dangerous.

Investment: (Rates vary in each state) Pre-Licensing class $500. (Usually 2 days). License Applications: *Runners License $233* (Works for a professional bondsman) *Surety Bonds License $313* (A **surety bond** is **defined** as a contract among at least three parties: *the obligee* - the party who is the recipient of an obligation, *the principal* - the primary party who will perform the contractual obligation & *the surety* - who assures the obligee that the principal can perform the task.)

GATE KEY

Exam: State Bail bond License exam. (To be taken after successful completion of pre-licensing course.) Your course instructor will tell you where to register for the exam. The exam usually cost $51.50 depending on your state.

Music Producer

Gate Keys

1. Image
2. Character
3. Hard Work and Determination
4. Qualifications and Certifications
5. Good Credit
6. No Criminal Record
7. Clean Driving Record

Estimated Salary: $20,000 - $6,000,000 a year

Certifications: Business License, Corporation, Tax ID Number.

Required age to start: 13 (optional)

The music producer profession can pay dividends early, if you go about it the right way. The biggest misconception is that producers only really get paid when they make it big. If you're serious about being a music producer, first you must learn the art of music. Some people have the innate ability to piece together some spectacular scores of music. Others need to train by taking band in school to begin perfecting their craft. In any event all producers must go through this stage whether band, basement or beating on the kitchen table. Consistent practice will hone your craft and get you headed in the right direction.

GATE KEY

Producers eat, sleep and breathe music. If your every moment doesn't consist of making music or thinking about your next beat, then maybe this isn't for you!

Kanye West, Swizz Beats, T-Pain, Dr. Dre, Shawty Redd, Neptunes, Cool and Dre, Dungeon Family are just a few of the producers that took their hunger for music and made it pay millions! Every last one of them didn't give a damn about what anyone thought about their style of music. They just stuck to their dream and kept creating. If you want to be successful at this game, then you will have to do the same. The very first thing that you need to do is perfect your craft, make beats until that's all you hear in your head every day, no matter if you're walking to your next class or eating lunch, you need to become that producer that you're dreaming about and the only way to do that is to get to it!

Tools: Your studio, bedroom, basement, garage or what have you, should consist of any instruments you play: speakers, keyboards, digital drum machine, DJ equipment (i.e. Turn tables, CD-J's), recording booth, mixing board, microphones, recording software, computers, CD burner, couch, bed and a small fridge. You should be spending a lot of time in this room. This is where your dreams will be created and leaving should be the last thing on your mind!

Funding: You will need money to upgrade your equipment; this is where honing your craft starts to pay off. Create some fliers and promote studio time in one hour blocks and start selling your beats for a small fee as well. Target your peers in school and the neighborhood. Doing this will build your income and your producer image at the same time. Charge a set fee for 3-hour recording session or by the hour. It's your business, so you should set a fair price. Remember you're not big time yet, so don't get greedy! Those same customers may want to buy some of your beats, so always play some for them while they're in the studio with you. Now, if you have any kind of business savvy, charge them to put their tracks to CD. Remember you should also have that CD burner.

During a daily business transaction, you should have sold studio time, some beats, burnt some CD's and if they buy some beats, then you will be getting some free promotion as well. After all, it will be your music that they will be singing or rapping over!

Team: You should also be thinking about a team to help you promote your new music producer image and business. Build your own team of artists to help promote the tracks. Make some hot beats, put your team on the tracks, drop it on CD then put it on the streets to get a buzz going. Please don't forget to put your contact information on your CD's and also have your team to drop a plug (shout out) over the track. Create a trademark saying or logo, so that people will know it's you. (Always make sure that the local club and radio DJ's get free promo copies.)

GATE KEY

Internet Cash: Upload your tracks (mix tape) to iTunes and to any other online medium that you can find and sell your music for a small fee. You may also choose to release some tracks for free just to get your name out there. Create you a simple music video to upload to You Tube. This will also help to build your fan base. Soulja Boi and Justin Bieber got both their starts via You Tube and now they're making millions.

Record Label: If you're lucky and your team just happened to be hot enough to create a hit, you will have a record label situation on your hands. Please believe that if you're hot, the right people will come looking for you, I can guarantee you that. Just don't play yourself when they come! The smart thing to do would be to get a distribution deal to distribute your music. You will make the most money in the end doing it that way. Bad Boy, Cash Money, Def Jam, Roc, Grand Hustle all started with distribution deals to name a few.

License: You will need a business license, if you plan on selling your beats and studio time. You don't want to make it big and the IRS come knocking years later. All of your licenses can be obtained at your County Clerk's Office and TAX ID Numbers from the IRS.

Custom Auto Painter

Gate Keys

1. **Image**
2. **Character**
3. **Hard Work and Determination**
4. **Qualifications and Certifications**
5. Good Credit
6. No Criminal Record
7. Clean Driving Record

Estimated Salary: $20,000 - $100,000 a year

Certifications: Business License, Corporation, Tax ID Number, Internship.

Required age to start: 15 (optional)

If you love the idea of painting cars, bikes and trucks to turn them into works of art then this is the profession for you. Millions of vehicle owners take pride in their automobiles. One of the most important things to them will always be a super bad, hot rod paint job! As a custom auto painter you will have the opportunity to show off your artistic painting skills, whether it be a nice candy paint finish, an awesome mural, a flip flop or maybe just a clean basic detailed finish.

The owner of that automobile will be counting on you to make their baby look good. If your high school offers auto paint vocational classes, sign up in a hurry.

Training: Take all classes pertaining to custom auto painter, if it's offered in your school. Find a job at a local custom auto paint shop, intern if you must. The experience will be worth more than the money during this early stage.

Options: Once you've mastered the craft and completed enough jobs to build a great customer base while working at the shop, you may choose to branch off and open your own. After a while your work will start to speak for itself then you can charge whatever price you want, if you're good enough.

Your Shop: Depending on your location you may find a great space such as a warehouse, garage, previously owned shop or someone willing to lease or share a shop with you. Whatever the case, get in there and set up shop accordingly then get the word out to your customer base. It will also be a good idea to do some advertising to let people know that you are open for business.

License: Business license can be obtained from your local County Clerk's Office. Tax ID from the IRS.

Model

Gate Keys

1. Image
2. Character
3. Hard Work and Determination
4. Qualifications and Certifications
5. Good Credit
6. No Criminal Record
7. Clean Driving Record

Estimated Salary: $20,000 - $2,000,000 a year

Certifications: Great looks and drive to succeed.

Required age to start: 13 (optional)

The modeling profession is both unique and challenging. It's one of the few that offers a career based solely on your looks. Of course some training will be needed to perfect the craft, but that's something any seasoned model can teach you. Be it Iman, Cyndi Crawford, Tyson, Tyra Banks or Naomi most experienced models can teach you the craft, but be warned, it will be a tedious journey. If you are 100 percent sure that you want to be a model, the following will come in handy.

Duties: Models are most often used to promote a product or brand. This can be done in a few ways: modeling for magazines, on billboards, fliers or posters are called *print modeling*. If you participate in modeling designer's clothing on the cat walk, that's considered *runway* modeling. When modeling or selling brands in TV commercials, you will be a part of a *Television Ad Campaign*. Promoting a product during a trade show or event is usually called a *gig* because it's only temporary, lasting a few hours or just a day or two. It should also be noted that this profession has places for *hand models, foot models, mouth models, hair models and teeth models* to name a few. Think about some commercials or ads that you have seen that only use one body part.

Schools: If you desire, you may elect to go to a local modeling school to learn the basics about your craft. Every city has a few modeling schools that usually has some kind of package that you can purchase where they will teach you how to walk, dress, talk, eat, etc. This is optional and totally up to you and maybe your parents, depending on your age.

Struggle: Like any other profession this too has its ups and downs. There are millions of women and men that aspire to be models and most of them won't make it. To have a fighting chance you will have to put in 120% every day and do whatever it takes to make it.

Diet: The majority of models will have to stay in shape. This means working out daily and having a great diet. Remember your body is your resume, so watch what you eat because not doing so will definitely ruin your chances.

Photos: Every model should have at least two great photographers on speed dial. You will need someone that knows how to shoot you and capture your best features. Keep your head shots fresh and readily available. These will be required for every job to which you apply. In the business they're called comp cards and are usually submitted along with a resume of your accomplishments.

Image: Models should be able to switch up their image at any given moment. After all that's really what a model does, adapting his/her look to promote an image, clothing and or product to the masses.

Agency: In order to make a living at this profession, you will need an agent. Your agent will be responsible for sending you to castings for upcoming gigs, commercials, print ads, etc. However, it will be your responsibility to book the gig or campaign. So bring you're A-Game because I promise that you probably won't be the only model there. Search for a Modeling Agency in your city, do your homework on them to see if they can offer you what you're looking for, then set up a meet.

Make sure you view their web site, check the reviews and most importantly check their client base to see if they represent any companies for whom you would like to model. If not, then this isn't the company for you. I suggest you keep looking and even move to a new city where it's more promising, if needed!

GATE KEY

Once you find an Agency that you like and they like you, be sure to have a lawyer review your modeling contract with you. Inquire about anything that you don't like or understand. Remember your goal is to make a living doing this, so make sure that the money will be distributed and split properly.

Location: New York, London, California, Atlanta, Miami and Paris. These are the locations that hold the most opportunity for you as a model, male or female. At the end of the day your dream should lead you to get work in all of the above locations. If this is not your focus then maybe you should realign your dreams or dream bigger!

Casting calls: A casting call is where models go to audition for an upcoming job. Your agent will give you a date, time and location. It will be up to you to show up and show out. This is where all the training, photos and dreams meet. If you impressed the casting director, they will call your agent to request a second meet or offer you the job. So again, always bring you're A-Game! If there is a script, make sure you practice it over and over again for several days and the night before!

Cash Flow: With a great agent and great work ethic, you should have plenty of opportunities to land several big campaigns and contracts that pay very well. This may sound easy, but I promise you that it isn't. You will be competing with models just as hungry as you are, if not hungrier. Just remember that the sky is the limit and don't be afraid to take a chance, it's the only way that you will know if you can make it.

GATE KEY

Social Media Promoter

Gate Keys

1. **Image**
2. **Character**
3. **Hard Work and Determination**
4. Qualifications and Certifications
5. Good Credit
6. No Criminal Record
7. Clean Driving Record

Estimated Salary: $20,000 - $100,000 a year

Certifications: Business License, Tax ID Number.

Required age to start: 13 (optional)

The SMP is a fairly new profession that was created from the emergence of social networking mediums. These mediums now allow us to get information in seconds where as it took days and sometimes weeks to get the same data in the past. It really all began when we started using our emails to e-vite and/or promote an event to our friends, family and colleagues through email blast.

With the popularity of Blackberries and Smart Phones years ago that allowed us to get emails to our mobile devices, this proved to be a successful way of promoting. The only caveat with the email method was that the messages could sometimes go to our junk mail or spam folders which meant we wouldn't receive them immediately or never at all, if we didn't check our spam folders.

Now that we have faster information mediums such as Twitter, Instgram and Facebook to name the more popular, the digital method of promoting is both instantaneous and vivid with the ability to post digital fliers, photos and videos within a second. The secret to this profession, however, is not the speed of the post, but the number of followers you have. So the old saying about having a valuable network still rings true in this instance. A SMP with 1 million followers, fans or friends can charge more than a SMP with just 20 thousand followers. The objective here is to charge your potential customer a set amount to promote their event to your network. If your base responds to the post that you advertise, then you should impact the event that you're promoting.

This is where you make your bones. If all goes well with the social promotion campaign, this will result in repeat customers and it will also help you attract new ones. Many of you reading this may very well have half the battle won already by the number of followers you have. I bet you didn't know how valuable they were until now, did you? I've included some tips below to help you turn your social network into a business. Good luck and have fun!

Business Name: Come up with a catchy name for your SMP business.

GATE KEY

Paypal Account: You will need this to collect payment for your services. It's easy to send a Paypal invoice via email.

Followers: Build a network of followers that will be likely candidates for the type of business or events you plan to promote. Location is really important if you plan to market events in your area. It doesn't make since to have 50,000 followers that live in New York and you're promoting events in LA! Then again this depends on what you're promoting.

Pricing: I recommend posting 3 times a day. Morning, Afternoon and Evening, seven days a week! For example, you may charge $50 a post and offer a discount if they purchase six during that week. Remember that one post a day will not be effective as 6 a day, the more posts you promote the better as long as it's strategized and doesn't overwhelm your followers. If your customer really wants to maximize your services, discuss a promotion plan with them; first, on time followed by days to advertise.

You should also offer a price for live promotion-- meaning you or your team will promote live videos and pictures while at the event. This will entice your followers to come out and join the event when they see you interacting. I would charge double for this type of promotion or include it in a package deal.

After Party Images: Always post after event images the next day. This will help build your clientele data base of event images on your social networks (stock footage) and will also have people talking the next day. Those who attended will share your photos of them and those who didn't attend will be envious. You should provide a price for this as well or include it in a package deal.

Business License: You will need a Business License for this profession, if you will be charging a fee for your services. This is important because some of your clients will file your invoice with their accountant for business tax purposes and you will want to be legit. Since this is a new profession, I would get a business license in the marketing category when visiting the County Clerk's Office. Your Tax ID number can be obtained from the IRS.

Airline Pilot

Gate Keys

1. Image
2. Character
3. Hard Work and Determination
4. Qualifications and Certifications
5. Good Credit
6. No Criminal Record
7. Clean Driving Record

Estimated Salary: $32,000 - $200,000 a year

Certifications: Airline Transport Pilot Certificate (ATP)

Required age to start: 16 (optional)

Now is the perfect time to start training to be a pilot, if you're still in high school. To get started you should visit your local airport and ask to take an introductory ride. The rides don't usually cost a whole lot and you will also get to fly the airplane. Once you've completed this task and you still have the urge to be a pilot then this is something I recommend that you pursue. So, get focused and take advantage of the following information.

Ground School: Before you start taking flying lessons you should take a ground school course. Ask your local airport if they offer one or know of anyone that does. In ground school you will begin learning the basics of this profession. If there is not a ground school offered in your area, get a few books on pilot ground schooling and learn all you can prior to signing up for Flight School.

Flying Hours: The FAA requires that a pilot complete 1500 hours total as a pilot before receiving an ATP Certificate. Once you start flight school you will be on your way to accumulating these hours. So find a school as soon as a possible and get started.

Military Pilot: After completing your flight school and 1500 hours, you may choose to be a Military Pilot. Your ATP certification will help you acquire the honorable position of a military pilot, if you choose to join. It should also be noted that pilots with military experience are highly recruited by the major airlines.

Private Pilot: Your ATP will allow you to fly for any private airline. This also includes Corporate, Agriculture and Regional Aviation. Your certification gives you permission to fly for hire.

FAA requirements for U.S Airline Captains: 1). A pilot must have a minimum of 1000 flight hours as a co-pilot in air carrier operations prior to serving as a captain for a U.S Airline. 2). Enhanced training requirements for an ATP certificate, including 50 hours of multi-engine flight experience and completion of a new FAA-approved training

GATE KEY

program. 3). An allowance for pilots with fewer than 1500 hours of flight time or who have not reached the minimum age of 23 to obtain a "restricted privileges" ATP certificate. A restricted privileges ATP certificate allows a pilot to serve as a co-pilot until he or she obtains the necessary 1500 hours. If you have not yet reached the age of 23, you still may fly as co-pilot if you fall in one of the following categories:

- Military pilots with 750 hours total time as a pilot,
- Pilots who are at least 21 years old with 1500 flight hours.

FAA Rules for U.S Airline Captains:

1. Airline Transport Pilot (ATP) Certificate--multi-engine airplane.

    - At least 23 years old.
    - Hold commercial pilot certificate with instrument training.
    - Pass ATP knowledge and practical test.
    - 1500 hours total time as pilot.
    - Have at least 50 hours in a multi-engine airplane.
    - Successfully complete new ATP certification training program prior to taking the ATP knowledge test.

2. Airline Transport Pilot certificate with restricted privileges (multi-engine airplane rating only).

    - At least 21 years old.

- Hold commercial pilot certificate with instrument rating.
- Successfully complete new ATP certification training program prior to taking the ATP knowledge test.
- Pass ATP knowledge and practical test.
- At least 750 hours total time as military pilot or 1500 total time as a pilot.

GATE KEY

Disc Jockey aka DJ

Gate Keys

1. **Image**
2. **Character**
3. **Hard Work and Determination**
4. **Qualifications and Certifications**
5. **Good Credit**
6. No Criminal Record
7. Clean Driving Record

Estimated Salary: $50,000 - $2,000,000 a year

Certifications: Natural love of music and interacting with people.

Required age to start: 16 (optional)

    All of our lives have been influenced and for some still is being influenced by the DJ! Whether you're listening to the radio while in traffic, at work, in the club, restaurant, at home or just during your everyday leisure, at some point you move to the beat of the DJ. Disc Jockeys come with colorful street names, unique images and voices and most of all a Big Love for music. Every city and town, small or large has their own network of DJ's. Whether it's radio jockeys, club DJ's or just DJ's for hire, the DJ profession is big business.

Gate Keys Hard work and Determination along with Image require more than extra dedication when it comes to this profession. Anyone can play music, but it takes a crafty individual to network with others and demand attention while spinning and promoting music. The DJ is the gate keeper to the next hit. They are responsible for spinning the records in the clubs and on radio, which in turn drives sales for the artist. So it's imperative that the DJ stay abreast of all the latest trends of music as well as what the streets are saying about the next hottest album and or artist. Before we continue with how to get started in this profession, ask yourself one thing, *"Do I love music?"* If the answer is yes, then read on; if not, I suggest you turn the page because this profession will require every second of your time and energy, if you plan to make a ton of money doing it.

Music: Music comes in all types of genres. Most Dj's choose two to three and stick with those, but a Great DJs can spin any music at any time and in any place. It doesn't matter if you decide to spin Country, Hip Hop, R&B, Dancehall, Gospel, Reggae, Blues, Old School, Jazz, Rock & Roll, Pop or Disco there will be a market for you to flourish in this profession.

Craft: You must practice at this profession like any other one, if you plan to become great at it. Learn all you can about the artist and their music no matter what genre you pursue. It's important that you study their fan base as well because you will play a big part in getting their music to the people. This is paramount to your success as a DJ. Why you ask? Because those same people will follow you to all of your events and parties to show their support for you and the music you play. This is the essence of your network; this is where you build your net worth. So, study everything about being a DJ and the music that you will be playing. Start building your music library now and always remember, once a hit always a hit!

Mediums: I can remember back in the 70's when I was coming up. My parent's music came on 8-track tapes and reel to reels. The music codes were embedded on tape or ribbon back then and you could only get so many plays out of the reel or 8-track before the ribbon stretched or popped. The other popular medium was the album or as we called it-- wax! The album came in 12-inch vinyl and 45 aka the smaller version.

We would play these albums on our record players, but like its predecessors it was also flawed. After a period of time the albums would get scratched causing the music to skip a groove or two on the vinyl album making the needle jump from one song verse to the other. Man that was annoying! Then came the smaller version of the 8-track and reel to reel. This was the cassette tape. The cassette had two sides, a side A and side B. Each side was 30 to 45 minutes long which made more space for more music.

Along with the vinyl records and the emergence of the cassette tape in the mid 80's the mix-tape was born. DJ's from New York, Miami, California and

Atlanta would record their radio shows, parties and special music collaborations onto the long cassette tapes then sell them to anyone that would buy it. On the underground scene this became the vehicle to promote both the DJ and the artist's new music; DJ's would drop shout outs on the cassettes to further promote themselves and the music to the streets.

At the end of the 80's and early nineties the CD aka Compact Disc hit the scene. This would change the game and take the industry to new heights, for better or for worse. The CD had a longer shelf life than both the vinyl and cassette, plus it could hold more music. But, the one caveat to the Compact Disc was that if it got scratched, it wasn't good anymore! The dang thing wouldn't even play sometimes and to make it worse, many DJ's tried to incorporate it into their sets and use CD's in place of albums, but it was a headache. Can you imagine a club full of people on the dance floor jamming and the dang CD scratches and stops the whole party! Yep, that used to happen! Thank God for Napster, mp3's, Apple and good ole' technology.

The profession had a few bumps in the road, but managed to maintain through it all. Today because of that flawed history we have the CDJ's in many formats, which I think is awesome. No more scratched CD's, no more carrying around crates and crates of albums or CD's unless you just want to! We live in a digital age and the DJ more than anyone has benefitted from the change, in my opinion.

GATE KEY

Club DJ: The sole purpose of the club disc jockey is to keep the party hype and the dance floor packed. Your catalog must consist of hits from the past to the present. You will earn your bones when you master this ability. Not everyone has the ear to mix the right beats per second in an arrangement that will keep the energy going. This comes with hours and hours of practice along with a dying love for the craft. Several of my friends are full time Club DJ's and they make a very decent living at it. The sky really is the limit when it comes to your earning potential; just make sure that you're in a market where you can get plenty of work. If you're at the top of your game like you are supposed to be, you will need a booking manager and a street team to help you promote and keep up with your gigs.

Radio Jock: In today's market the radio DJ does more than spin records. They have their own radio show which will consist of a 4-hour block. This show can consist of just one DJ and sometimes up to 4 host jocks. Just turn on your local radio station and you will see what I mean. Some of the shows are local and some are syndicated (broadcast nationally). There are many perks as a radio jock. For example: you will get booked at more events, you get to meet a lot of recording artists, producers, music execs and other celebs, you will have a huge fan base because of the show and more.

 This is definitely a situation where you will need a street team and a manager to help you capitalize on your success as a radio personality. But, don't get it twisted, you will have to work hard to get this position; most radio jocks work their way up as interns at the radio station before they get their chance and you will not be any different. So get ready to put in the work--for free! (Sacrifice is the price we pay for Success.)

Group DJ: Every music artist needs a DJ. In this position you will travel with the group whether on tour, at the club, rehearsal, etc. During concerts you will be responsible for hyping up the crowd before the group hits the stage and spinning during the show sometimes as well. Yes, you will experience all of the groupie love along with the Artist. Aside of that you will also get booked to spin at clubs and other events because of that fame. So keep a booking manager close by. Most of the time the group's manager and street team will support you as well.

It is important to remember that you will be representing the group that you spin for at all times, so don't do anything foolish to jeopardize the brand. The main objective is to get money and have fun doing it!

A Great DJ: A great DJ will be able to perform at all of the above levels of the profession. Make it your duty to perfect each and every level and make allies in the process. Disc Jockeys should always stick together; this will expand your opportunities along with your net worth!

GATE KEY

Politician

Gate Keys

1. Image
2. Character
3. Hard Work and Determination
4. Qualifications and Certifications
5. Good Credit
6. No Criminal Record
7. Clean Driving Record

Estimated Salary: $50,000 - $570,000 a year

Certifications: U.S Citizen

Required age to start: 18

One of the biggest misconceptions in American politics is that you need a Law Degree to run for any political office. When the truth is that you don't need a degree at all for most office positions. At least three of our past Presidents didn't have a college degree. All politicians are elected by the people. It is up to the politician, however, to campaign and win those votes. This is no easy task by any means; it will take all 7 gate keys ten times over to be successful in this profession. Let's put it in perspective. To run for office you will need thousands of votes, which means you will have to be constantly in the public eye and have a good name in the State, City, Precinct, Region and or County depending on for which seat you're running.

A great politician should take his/her office seriously as well as the commitments made to the people. Too often, honesty falls to the wayside when juxtapose to lobbyists and their agendas. It will take a person with a devotion to a set of core beliefs to win the vote of the people. At least that's the way it should be! In any event this is a profession you can start grooming for while in high school. You can run for class President, treasury, etc. Once you're at the legal age to work, you may try interning at one of your local political offices in town to get your feet wet and start building your name. This is where the road to your first political campaign will begin. Each office has a minimum starting age with the lowest being 18. Below you will find the qualifications for the political offices that don't require you to have a degree:

1. **President**: Minimum age is 35, must be born in the United States, must be a U.S Citizen for 14 years, must be a registered voter, a term in office is 4 years and there is a 2-term limit.
2. **U.S House of Representatives**: Minimum age is 25, must be a State Resident for at least 1 day, must be a U.S Citizen for 7 years, must be a registered voter, a term in office is 2 years and there is no limit on terms.
3. **Governor**: Minimum age is 30, must be a State Resident for at least 7 years, must be a U.S Citizen for 10 years, must be a registered

voter, a term in office is 4 years and there is a 2-term limit.
4. **Lt. Governor**: Minimum age is 30, must be a State Resident for at least 7 years, must be a U.S Citizen for 10 years, must be a registered voter, a term in office is 4 years and there is a 2-term limit.
5. **U.S Senate**: Minimum age is 30, must be a State Resident for at least 1 day, must be a U.S Citizen for 9 years, must be a registered voter, a term in office is 6 years and there is no limit on terms.
6. **Secretary of State**: Minimum age is 25, must be a State Resident for at least 5 years, must be a U.S Citizen for 7 years, must be a registered voter, a term in office is 4 years and there is a 2-term limit.
7. **Attorney General**: Minimum age is 25, must be a State Resident for at least 5 years, must be a U.S Citizen for 7 years, must be a registered voter, a term in office is 4 years and there is a 2-term limit.
8. **State Auditor**: Minimum age is 25, must be a State Resident for at least 5 years, must be a U.S Citizen for 7 years, must be a registered voter, a term in office is 4 years and there is a 2-term limit.
9. **State Treasurer**: Minimum age is 25, must be a State Resident for at least 5 years, must be a U.S Citizen for 7 years, must be a registered voter, a term in office is 4 years and there is a 2-term limit.

10. **Commissioner of Agriculture and Industry**: Minimum age is 25, must be a State Resident for at least 5 years, must be a U.S Citizen for 7 years, must be a registered voter, a term in office is 4 years and there is a 2-term limit.
11. **Public Service Commission**: Minimum age is 18, must be a State Resident for at least 1 day, must be a U.S Citizen for 1 day, must be a registered voter, a term in office is 4 years and there is no limit on terms.
12. **State Board of Education**: Minimum age is 18, must be a State Resident for at least 1 day, must be a U.S Citizen for 1 day, must be a registered voter, a term in office is 4 years and there is no limit on terms.
13. **State Senate**: Minimum age is 25, must be a State Resident for at least 3 years, must be a U.S Citizen for 1 day, must be a registered voter, a term in office is 4 years and there is no limit on terms. (Must be a resident of the district for one year prior to the election.)
14. **State House of Representatives**: Minimum age is 21, must be a State Resident for at least 3 years, must be a U.S Citizen for 1 day, must be a registered voter, a term in office is 4 years and there is no limit on terms. (Must be a resident of the district for one year prior to the election.)
15. **Probate Judge**: Minimum age is 18, must be a State Resident for at least 1 year, must be a U.S Citizen for 1 day, must be a registered voter, a term in office is 6 years and there is no limit on terms. (Must have resided in the

district which candidate seeks to represent for one year prior to election. No one may be elected or appointed to a judicial office after reaching the age of 70.)

16. **Circuit Clerk**: Minimum age is 18, must be a State Resident for at least 1 day, must be a U.S Citizen for 1 day, must be a registered voter, a term in office is 6 years and there is no limit on terms.
17. **Sheriff**: Minimum age is 18, must be a State Resident for at least 1 day, must be a U.S Citizen for 1 day, must be a registered voter, a term in office is 4 years and there is no limit on terms.
18. **County Board of Education**: Minimum age is 18, must be a State Resident for at least 1 day, must be a U.S Citizen for 1 day, must be a registered voter, a term in office is 4 or 6 years and there is no limit on terms. (Must be a resident of the district for one year prior to the election.)
19. **County Commission**: Minimum age is 18, must be a State Resident for at least 1 day, must be a U.S Citizen for 1 day, must be a registered voter, a term in office is 4 or 6 years and there is no limit on terms. (Must be a resident of the district for one year prior to the election. If representing a specific district, must be a resident of the district for at least one year prior to date of taking office.)
20. **Mayor**: Minimum age is 18, must be a State Resident for at least 90 days, must be a U.S Citizen for 1 day, must be a registered voter, a

term in office is 4 years and there is no limit on terms. (Must be a resident of the City for 90 days prior to the election.)
21. **City Council**: Minimum age is 18, must be a State Resident for at least 90 days, must be a U.S Citizen for 1 day, must be a registered voter, a term in office is 4 years and there is no limit on terms. (Must be a resident of the City for 90 days prior to the election.)
22. **City Commission**: Minimum age is 18, must be a State Resident for at least 90 days, must be a U.S Citizen for 1 day, must be a registered voter, a term in office is 4 years and there is no limit on terms. (Must be a resident of the City for 90 days prior to the election.)

**Always check your State Qualifications for any changes before consideration.

GATE KEY

Film/Video Producer

Gate Keys

1. Image
2. Character
3. Hard Work and Determination
4. Qualifications and Certifications
5. Good Credit
6. No Criminal Record
7. Clean Driving Record

Estimated Salary: $20,000 - $2,000,000 a year

Certifications: Corporation, Business License, Tax ID Number, Video Production Courses.

Required age to start: Varies

The art of film and video production has changed over the years. Not to the point where you no longer need a camera, but in relation to the technology and speed aspect of initial shooting to completion production. Cameras are everywhere now and they come in thousands of styles and sizes. With the emergence of You Tube, Facebook, Twitter and Instagram providing immediate exposure to the world as new vehicles to showcase your films and videos, it just makes this profession that much more gratifying.

High School Courses: If your school offers a course on film and video production, you should enroll as soon as you can. The earlier the better! The whole idea of making a movie or video may seem glamorous; it is anything but. It not only involves the recording aspect of the profession, but the editing, scripting, casting, etc. The behind the scenes work of video production is very tedious, but is a necessary evil. If you find yourself not wanting to participate in the behind the scenes department of film and video production, you can always hire someone to edit, cast, etc.

If your school doesn't offer any courses, you can purchase a camera and some video production software to get you started. Watch some how-to videos on using the equipment then go at it the hard way! This may not be in a classroom setting, but I assure you that it will get the job done when it comes to getting experience.

Cameras: When choosing a camera, be sure that it has all the capabilities that you need to get the job done. If you can't afford to buy a camera at the time, you can always rent what you need until you earn the money to buy one. There are several great companies that make movie cameras. Sony, Canon, Samsung are just a few that stock cameras for video and film producers. Since you're just starting out you may want something less expensive, but if you have the money, I say go for the best! Just remember that the camera doesn't make a great film, it's the guys and gals behind the camera writing the story that make the magic happen. The camera is only the tool used to get a story to its audience.

Software: The most important piece of software that you will own as a producer is your editing software. You will use this to piece your story together frame by frame, add graphics, sound, time codes and more.

You can edit your film on your PC or Mac. This will be a choice that you will have to make and remember that the software is not interchangeable between the two systems. There are hundreds of companies that make editing software. I suggest you do your due diligence when searching for a brand that will fit your liking the best.

Your Production Company: Before you start taking on projects to build your name and gain experience. I strongly recommend you come up with a business name and create a logo for your company. You will eventually be charging for your services so a Tax ID number will be necessary as well as a business license. The license can be obtained from the County Clerk's Office and the Tax ID from the IRS.

Crew: Once you figure the production out, you will soon see that a crew is paramount. Directors, make-up artists, producers and grips to name a few, are key players in this profession.

Recording High School & Local Events: This is where you will build your brand. So take extra precautions to create a great product before you release it to your peers. You only get one chance to make a first impression, so make all of the hard work count!

During high school there are several events, games, functions, etc. that you can record, edit and release as a project. For example, there are: talent shows, marching bands, cheerleading competitions, sports highlight reels, games, pep rallies, speaking engagements, plays, church events, weddings, etc. Take advantage of as many of these activities as you can. If you create a great product, your work and brand will start to demand attention with several requests for work.

Keep in mind that local TV stations use high school sports footage every weekend, so why not be that company providing the highlight reels for your school?

You should also find local events in your town and/or neighborhood to record. Take every opportunity to build your resume, brand and catalogue.

Music Videos: Every high school has their own set of entertainers. Seek them out and offer to put them on camera. What up-and-coming artist doesn't want to star in her very own music video?! Expand this service to other artists in your city, town and neighborhood as well. But whatever you do, please make sure that you have the editing process down completely before attempting to shoot a music video. I can tell you from experience that this can be a headache, if you don't have it all together. If you're not comfortable with editing, recruit someone that is. Synching music, dancing, scripting and timing is no joke.

Short Films: A short film is a great way to start bringing your ideas to life. Create a story with some compelling characters, a great story line and great location then take on the challenge. The story really doesn't have to be yours; you can choose to shoot a film that one of your friends or crew members wrote. Since you're in charge, the choice is yours. Shoot as many of these as you can then critique them and take all comments and criticism into consideration. This is the only way that you will become better--persistent practice makes a perfect product.

Documentary: This is based from an actual or through re-creating an actual event, era, life story, etc. that purports to be factually accurate and contains no fictional elements.

Commercials: This is usually a 15-60 second scripted video designed to promote a certain product, individual or event. The time of the video depends on the vehicle used to promote it and the time slot allotted.

Movies: Producers inevitability want to make a movie for the big screen. Before you get to this point, however, you must master all areas of this profession or have a team in place who are experts in the fields that you aren't.

Filming for hire: Once you are confident in your abilities as a producer you are ready to make money! You may choose to charge by the hour or by the type of film you are producing, short film, documentary, commercial, video, etc. I suggest you do some research on pricing by seeing what your local competitors are charging. Keep in mind that you have a crew that will need to be paid also, so always factor their pay into your rates.

GATE KEY

Online Business Owner

Gate Keys

1. Image
2. Character
3. Hard Work and Determination
4. Qualifications and Certifications
5. Good Credit
6. No Criminal Record
7. Clean Driving Record

Estimated Salary: $20,000 - $2,000,000 a year

Certifications: Corporation, Business License, Tax ID Number.

Required age to start: Varies

One of the most intriguing things about the internet is its ability to make the world a smaller place. This makes it the perfect vehicle to touch billions of people and promote your products or services to them via an online business. This profession like many others requires hard work! You will need a domain name, a hosting company and a great marketing plan. You can build as many sites as you want and promote any product or service you want. The sky is the limit as long as you're willing to put in the work.

Domain Name & Hosting: There are hundreds of companies out there like Yahoo, Go Daddy and more that offer registration for your domain names as well as web hosting. I recommend you shop around for what fits you best.

Paypal: At the moment, Paypal is the leading merchant service for collecting and sending money securely online. You will need an account to collect your money via your site. Other merchants do exist and you should take a look at those as well.

Products: I would do some research before launching any product. Some things to consider are: your niche market, geographical location, cost, shipping and most importantly supply and demand.

Shipping: If you're going to ship products to your customer directly, you must take postage into consideration as it will affect your bottom line. Another option is to sell products through a third party for a commission where you get a percentage and they take care of the shipping for you. The choice is yours.

Search Engines: It's important to list your company with as many search engines as possible. If you can afford it, you should hire an SEO to help increase traffic to your business site.

Promoting: This is where you identify your customers then put a strategic marketing plan together to drive them to your site to induce sales. Be creative and aggressive in your approach!

GATE KEY

License: This all depends on the infrastructure of your business. You will need a Tax ID number, Business License and a Corporation to get started. License can be purchased from your local County Clerk's Office and Tax ID number from the IRS.

Floor Installation Company

Gate Keys

1. Image
2. Character
3. Hard Work and Determination
4. Qualifications and Certifications
5. Good Credit
6. No Criminal Record
7. Clean Driving Record

Estimated Salary: $20,000 - $200,000 a year

Certifications: Corporation, Business License, Tax ID Number.

Required age to start: 16

Installing carpet, tile and hardwood floors is a very lucrative business. But, it is one that makes you earn every penny. The good news is that it's a trade that can be easily learned, if you're willing. While in high school, you should get a job with a local company to get some hands-on experience laying floors. A few years doing so will give you the knowledge and training to start your own business, if you so desire. As an owner you can put in bids with home builders, government companies, apartment complexes and private business to put in their flooring. This is where you make the big bucks and build important business relationships. So pay close attention while you're an employee.

Insurance: You will need to purchase general liability insurance once you start your business. This protects your company and your clients, if any incidents occur while installing floors. It also guarantees your work making it 'bonded'. When placing bids for huge jobs, companies will require that you have insurance.

License: You will need a business license, corporation and Tax ID number. Business licenses can be obtained from your local County Clerk's Office and Tax ID numbers from the IRS.

Party Promoter

Gate Keys

1. Image
2. Character
3. Hard Work and Determination
4. Qualifications and Certifications
5. Good Credit
6. No Criminal Record
7. Clean Driving Record

Estimated Salary: $90,000 - $2,000,000 a year

Certifications: Corporation, Business License, Tax ID Number.

Required age to start: 16

Unlike the Club owner, the party promoter has free range. Your objective is to throw the hottest parties at the hottest venues in the city or in the world. That's right; *the world* is your playground! You don't necessarily need to promote parties only in your city. A great promoter will know when and where to throw a party. For example, any event that demands the masses is a perfect time and place to promote a party. Some events include: the Super Bowl, NBA Weekend, BET Awards, Oscars, Main Event Boxing Matches, Spring Break, Memorial Weekend, etc.

GATE KEY

(While in high school you will be limited to what events you can put on, but when you become of-age you will be well seasoned.) As a promoter it will be your responsibility to find a great venue in the area of the event, book it, put together a marketing plan, send out the street team, book a celebrity to host the party or just make an appearance if you desire, then watch the dollars roll in. This sounds easier than it looks, but it is very possible. It all starts at home; build your network and brand and please, save your money so you can invest in future ventures to keep your company going.

Crew: Your crew should consist of a personal assistant, bartender, security guards, street team, door person to collect the money and a good booking agent.

Street Team: The sole responsibility of your street team is to build your brand in the streets. It's imperative that you build strong credibility in the party promoter arena. You want to be known as the promoter that puts on the hottest parties, concerts and events! Every event you sponsor should be promoted using fliers, posters, word-of-mouth, social media, radio and TV if it's in your budget. Having a street presence will drive your brand home.

Bartender: If you're promoting an event to the 21 and over crowd, it's a good idea to have your own bartender. This will guarantee an accurate count of your bar sales, if you negotiated that in your event contract.

DJ's: Just like the club owner, as a promoter you will need to have several DJ's on your speed dial to use at your events. Having options will build your relationships among the DJ community and also gives you an array of talent from which to choose. Keep your options open because one jockey may be better suited for a party than another.

Venues: Promoters must scout all clubs and venues in the area to see if they are suited for an upcoming event. Get to know the club owners and managers; keep an eye on what nights are the busiest. This will put you in play for any future negotiations between the club and your company.

VIP Booths: Once you're of age, it will be a good idea to reserve VIP Booths at all the hottest clubs in your area on their hottest nights. They will come in handy when the street team and your crew are working a promotion campaign. At the end of the day the whole team can meet there then party hard while they're still promoting. (Make sure the team is wearing branded shirts, hats, etc.) The booths will also be good for entertaining any future partners or investors. This will also help build your brand as well because people will be watching and talking.

Models: Models, both guys and girls, are important in this business. Patrons will want to be where the hippest, sexiest and fashionable people are. You can recruit your own models or hire them through a local model agency. Plus they make for good photos along with the patrons. You can also use them to do promotions during the event.

Booking Agent: This person will be one of the most important people in your circle! Your booking agent should be able to book any artist, celebrity, etc. A good agent will call you and let you know when a celebrity will be in your area and available for appearances. On the same note, your agent should have great relationships with the celebrity managers. If the agent that you decide to work with can't make this happen, move on to the next. It doesn't matter where your agent is located just make sure that they can meet your needs. There are thousands of agencies out there; do your research then make the best decision.

Net Worth: Always have a set budget in place before you take on a new project. It's important that you do not exceed your budget because profit is the main objective. Building a healthy bank account will assure you the ability to proceed. Always set a budget and stay close to it as possible. The more events you promote the easier it will become as long as you watch the numbers. The admission that you charge for your events should always equate to a great profit margin and should also cover pay roll.

License: Your business license can be obtained from the County Clerk's Office and you can get your Tax ID number from the IRS.

Flight Attendant

Gate Keys

1. Image
2. Character
3. Hard Work and Determination
4. Qualifications and Certifications
5. Good Credit
6. No Criminal Record
7. Clean Driving Record

Estimated Salary: $40,000 - $100,000 a year

Certifications: Diploma, GED, Flight Attendant School.

Required age to start: 18 - 21

If you want to travel the world, meet new people, experience different foods, traditions and get paid for it, then this is the profession for you! A flight attendant's job is to make the customers feel safe and provide excellent customer service. The hours can be long, like 10-hour days and you will be away from home on a regular basis.

Qualifications: Most airlines have height requirements for safety reasons, so be sure to check when applying. The minimum age starts at 18 and you must have a diploma or GED. If hired by an airline, a 3-8 week training course will be provided. It will also be a good idea to have some kind of customer service experience when you apply.

New flight attendant hires go through a few months of training before moving up to "junior" flight attendants. As a junior you will be under close supervision and receive lower pay than your senior counter-parts. Once you make senior you will make more money and have more control over your hours.

How to Apply: Once you make the decision to move forward, find an airline that you want to work for and apply.

Perks: Attendants receive steeply discounted airline tickets for themselves and family members. A per diem is given for meals. Usually this is between $2 to $3 an hour depending on your domestic or international assignments.

The best perk of all? You get to travel the world and get paid for it!

In my opinion this is one of the most exciting careers you can get into right out of high school. Good luck and have fun!

Photographer

Gate Keys

1. **Image**
2. **Character**
3. **Hard Work and Determination**
4. **Qualifications and Certifications**
5. Good Credit
6. No Criminal Record
7. Clean driving Record

Estimated Salary: $30,000 - $80,000 a year

Certifications: A love for the craft and a great eye!

Required age to start: Varies

Being a professional photographer requires a lot of time behind the camera. You will need to develop an eye for great art. The best way to get the experience is to start shooting any and everything. This is where you will find your eye (!)--the type of photography at which you're best.

While in high school, you should shoot games, talent shows, year book event photos, newspaper photos and whatever else you can. Remember you will need all the experience you can get behind the camera to prepare you for a successful career and it will look great in your portfolio. The lessons and knowledge you'll gain along the way will be priceless.

GATE KEY

Cameras: Cameras come in different sizes and shapes along with several accessories. Lights, lenses, flashes, tripods and more can be used with your cameras. Sony, Canon, Nikon and Olympus or among the top brands in photography; depending on your field of photography a specific brand may work better for you.

Salary: As a photographer you can earn money by working for a company making hourly pay. You can work freelance where you sell your photos for a fee to a buyer or for-hire where you charge by the hour.

Fashion Photography: If you have an eye for fashion and models, then you will love this sector of your profession. Photographers play a big role in promoting the fashion designer's clothes and accessories to the public through the photos they take. To maximize your earning potential in this sector, you should go where the market is flourishing. To date those markets are New York, Los Angeles, Miami, Atlanta and Paris. These locations host a steady diet of fashion shows and ad campaigns. You will need to build a relationship with the model agencies and fashion companies that have offices in these very locations because the majority of your money will come from them.

Sports Photography: The billion dollar industry of sports relies heavily on photographers. Your photos make up sports magazines, newspapers, posters, sports TV networks, ball cards and much more. No matter the city or state where you reside, there will be a market for sports photographers. Take advantage of your high school years and shoot as many games and sporting events as you can. Submit some of those photos to your local newspapers, news channels and sports networks. Start building your relationships, network and net worth now!

News Photographer: Every news channel needs good photographers on their payroll. Find opportunities to shoot local events that are news worthy then submit them to your local news station.

Crime Scene Photographer: Law enforcement relies heavily on photos to work their cases when it comes to solving crimes. If you have the stomach to shoot crime scene photos, go for it. You should contact your local police department about what procedures you need to take in this regard.

Celebrity Photographer: Also known as *The Paparazzi*, this type of photographer makes their money by selling photos of *celebrities* to the press, magazines, TV, etc. It takes a certain kind of individual to work this sector. In the entertainment business you are what we call a necessary evil. Your presence can be annoying at times, but the world is depending on you to get pictures of their favorite stars. The best opportunities are in New York, Hollywood, Atlanta, Las Vegas and Miami. To maximize your value, I suggest you work all the cities listed and the celebrity get-away spots.

Swim Suit Photographer: As a swim suit photographer you must have an eye for class and beauty. You will make your living shooting models for calendars, swim suit magazines and ad campaigns. Your earning potential will rely on relationships, quality of work, geographic location and an eye for talent.

Wedding Photographer: Establishing yourself as a great wedding photographer in your city or town can cement your career. It is important, however, to remember that referrals play a big part in this sector because of the intimate reactions you share while capturing family moments. Keep that in mind while you're smiling and shaking hands during the wedding and in between shots.

Family Portraits: This is one of the oldest sectors of photography and it doesn't get more cut-and-dry than this. You can charge families by the hour, session or look. Usually photographers will have a studio where they set appointments for shoots. As long as your work is good and prices are competitive you will be able to make money, if you stay consistent and work hard at it. Make sure, however, that you have a great marketing plan in place to draw in potential customers.

Copyrights: You will own rights to the photos you take unless you sign them over via a contract. Make sure you place your copyright on all of your work.

Contracts: Some of your customers will want to own their photos. You can choose to sell them the rights for a fee. Make sure it's written in the form of a contract that you both sign.

Limousine or Chauffer Service

Gate Keys

1. **Image**
2. **Character**
3. **Hard Work and Determination**
4. **Qualifications and Certifications**
5. **Good Credit**
6. No Criminal Record
7. **Clean Driving Record**

Estimated Salary: $90,000 - $1,000,000 a year

Certifications: Driver's License, Business License, Tax ID Number.

Required age to start: 17

With a valid driving license, nice car or SUV you can be in a great position to start a limo service. Thousands of people use chauffer type businesses on a daily basis. There are several reasons why someone may be in need of your services. It will be up to you to market your business to the public and private sectors. You should always wear a suit, tie and maybe a hat, if you like. Always dress professionally and present yourself as such. Below are some pointers to help you get started.

GATE KEY

Driver's License: You will need a valid driver's license before you get started.

Automobile: If you're in a situation where you can afford a nice luxury car or SUV, make sure that it is in good running condition. The heat and air must work and scheduled maintenance should be performed on a regular basis. You will want your customers to have the best experience ever! So go out of your way to make that happen!

Uniform: Standard dress for chauffer's is usually a black suit and tie with a white shirt and black hat. You may choose to go a different route and that's your choice, but whatever you do, keep it professional.

Marketing: You should target: airports, hotels, NBA arenas, NFL arenas, NHL arenas, MLB arenas, college arenas, wedding planners, bars, restaurants, etc. A website for your business will give you another platform to attract potential clients.

Infrastructure: Once you have chosen a name for your company and acquired all business licensing, you should decide on how many cars and drivers you want. This will give you a sense of direction and help you build your company.

Rates: Charging for your services can be done in a few different ways. *Hourly*: this is where you charge a set fee per hour. *Mileage*: you may charge a set fee for every mile that your company chauffeured the patron while in the limo. *Vehicle:* Each vehicle can be rated differently; for example, you can charge more for an SUV than a car.

License: Business license can be purchased at your local County Clerk's Office and your Tax ID number can be acquired from the IRS.

GATE KEY

Writer

Gate Keys

1. Image
2. Character
3. Hard Work and Determination
4. Qualifications and Certifications
5. Good Credit
6. No Criminal Record
7. Clean Driving Record

Estimated Salary: $20,000 - $2,000,000 a year

Certifications: English and Writing courses. Love of craft.

Required age to start: Varies

Becoming a professional writer will take a whole lot of training and dedication to the craft. Like anything you will need to practice at it every chance that you get. You can most definitely transition your high school education in this field to that of a pro, if you take all the necessary steps to get there. Writers have the option to go into several sectors. Those are: journalism, poetry, author, screen writer, song writer and editor. Each one of them play a very important part in today's society.

If you plan on making a decent earning in this field you will need to start early while in high school and work a part time job in the profession as well during the same time. The hands-on training and work ethic will enhance your skill set and put you on the right path. It is also important that you get involved with your school newspaper and any other activities that involve writing. When selecting your school courses, choose all of the writing classes available to you at that time. Take on the challenge, your career will depend on it.

Author: In my opinion this is the best part about being a writer. You get to create stories in your head then put them to paper and share them with the world. My favorite part is meeting the fans while attending book signings and other related events.

As a professional author your stories will be sold to the public through you or your publisher/distributor in the form of eBook, paperback and hardcovers.

Journalist: As a journalist your duty is to keep a record, diary or journal of daily events. These events can be written then sold to a publication, if you are working freelance. If employed by a company, the duties are the same, but your pay will be a salary. The events that you write about should be news worth, if not assigned by your employer. Some of the events may include: sports, politics, crime, entertainment, etc.

Potential employers can be magazines, newspapers, web sites, blogs, etc.

Screen Writer: Screen writers are responsible for creating great TV shows, movies, commercials and any project that may require your creative expertise. Writing school plays, talent show skits and more will polish your skills, but interning at a network in your city or town will put you on the right track. This will more than likely be a long process because you will be starting from the bottom, but the experience is priceless. When you deem yourself ready to take on this role, be sure to put in 110%.

Publisher: If you plan to go the traditional route as an author, you will need to find a publisher to represent you and distribute your work. This is usually a long and tedious process. Most publishing companies have set genres that they cater to and only have a limited amount of space on their current roster for any new talent. There is a submission process that you will need to follow when sending in your manuscript for consideration. Make sure that you follow the steps as required or it may delay your submission process and set you back months or even years.

When selecting a publisher, you should make sure that the company supports your style or genre. This is important because you don't want to waste any valuable time during this stage. Some publishers pay an advance if they plan to carry your title and some don't. If you get signed, this may be something that you will want to negotiate; remember, however, that it is an advance--meaning you will have to pay it back.

Smaller publishing companies don't usually offer advances, but will, however, have the same capabilities when it comes to getting your title to market. You should consider all of the above variables when searching for a publisher.

Self-Publish: In today's world of publishing, this process has become a whole lot easier than it was in the past. With the emergence of eBooks and digital presses offering print on demand (POD) services the market has changed tremendously. Today you can sell your books through millions of online stores and eReaders while cashing in on sales. Now you have the option to offer your book in any and all formats to the public. The POD process doesn't require a warehouse to store books before shipping. It simply prints the book on a digital press once it has been paid for and ordered. There are hundreds of companies out there that offer POD as well as eBook distribution. I suggest that you research them all then make your choice.

The eBook is the least expensive to produce. There is no printing cost involved leaving room for a huge profit. The eBook distributors like Amazon, Barnes & Noble, eBookit and Book Baby to name a few will pay you a percentage of your resale price, which is usually between 20%-70% depending on the listed price. Once you decide on an eBook distributor the company will explain the eBook production in detail.

The one caveat to self-publishing, however, is the editing process. There are a lot of books out on the market today that have not been properly edited.

GATE KEY

Because of this, some retailers shun titles that are self-published and will not sell them in their stores. If you decide to go this route, it will be well worth it to get your book edited before releasing it to market.

Song Writer: Song writers write for recording artists. Artists will pay you a fee for your song, if they like it then they add it to their catalogue of music. Most song writers are signed to record labels or industry managers that shop their songs to the artists and labels. You will also need to have your songs published through BMI, ASCAP or SESAC. These companies are used to publish music in the record industry.

ANTWAN BANK$

Staffing Agency

Gate Keys

1. Image
2. Character
3. Hard Work and Determination
4. Qualifications and Certifications
5. Good Credit
6. No Criminal Record
7. Clean Driving Record

Estimated Salary: $60,000 - $1,000,000 a year

Certifications: Business License, Tax ID Number, Business Owners Insurance.

Required age to start: 17

As a staffing agency your job will be to find talent or employees for your clients. Hiring the right employee can be a headache for some employers, if they don't have the time or infrastructure in place to do so. Taking on the staffing responsibilities for your client can save them time and money. Listed below are some important variables you'll need to know about starting a staffing agency:

Staffing: You will take on qualified candidates as employees to staff your clients open positions.

Because you are acting as the employee in this capacity, you will also be responsible for withholding income tax and paying workers compensation, disability and unemployment insurance.

Before starting your company you should take a look at some local staffing services to see how they hire and recruit talent as well as the starting pay they offer for positions. In most cases you will be able to negotiate starting salary with experienced employees.

Clients: These are the companies that will contract you to hire employees for their labor and expertise. You should be prepared to approach any company hiring in your area and offer them your services. A clean professional website should also be in place to attract potential clients and employees.

Contracts: This is where you implement your finders-fee for the talent you hire and the length of the contract. Some companies take a lump sum while others take their cut from every payroll. In any event this will be up to you and your client.

CPA: A certified professional accountant will be needed to keep your books and disburse payroll. Many entrepreneurs make the mistake of trying to run a financially based business without a CPA and find themselves in hot water. There are also payroll companies out there to assist you with this.

Insurance: Contact your local insurance agent and ask them about a business owner policy. You and your agent will discuss your business and decide what type of policy is best for you.

License: Business license can be obtained from the County Clerk's Office and your Tax ID number may be obtained from the IRS.

GATE KEY

Recording Artist

Gate Keys

1. **Image**
2. **Character**
3. **Hard Work and Determination**
4. **Qualifications and Certifications**
5. Good Credit
6. No Criminal Record
7. Clean Driving Record

Estimated Salary: $20,000 - $6,000,000 a year

Certifications: The desire to proceed along with natural talent and Vocal Training.

Required age to start: Varies

 Many dream about being a professional recording artist. In the past this dream was far away for many, but because of today's technology which includes, recording software, social media and the internet this dream is more obtainable than ever. It's still a long tedious process, but that's a small price to pay for your dream. The structure of the current market lends itself to your creativity and self-control. Image along with hard work and dedication are among the strongest of Gate Keys to be implemented in this profession.

Singer: Singing is not an art that you can teach. It's a God-given talent. If you plan to make a living as a vocalist, you should sing, sing, sing, sing every chance that you get to hone your craft. If you started singing before high school and kept it up, then you're in a good place. While in high school be sure to enroll in chorus and participate in any vocal events. Singing is just like any other profession, the more you practice at it, the better you'll get.

Rapper: Unlike singing, rapping is an art that you can learn. If this is your chosen profession, I suggest you study the history of rap and hip hop. Hopefully you will find your voice and begin to perfect your craft. Hip Hop is a way of life and has very heavy roots not to be confused with rap. I would start by researching from 1970 to the present to get a better understanding of the hip hop culture. This is important because what you stand for will be the foundation for your image. No one will support a fake artist.

Practice: Every waking moment, you should be thinking about becoming better at your craft. This means singing and or rapping every day while at home, school, work, subway, bus stop, etc. Use your phone, iPad, PC or whatever you need to record your voice then play it back and critique it. Do it again and again until you get better and better. Perform in front of an audience every chance that you get. Have a friend or family member critique it then use it to become better! *(Progressively practicing perfectly equals Professional.)*

GATE KEY

Image: Your image should attract fans, so think carefully about how you want to portray yourself. It's important to remember that your money will come from your fan base. Once you unleash your alter ego, it will be open to the world and whatever criticism they want to pour on the concept. The same is also true for acknowledgements. So, I'll say it again (!)-- put some deep thought into your image and what you'll release to the public.

Producer: Once you find your voice and image, the next step will be to find a producer whose style mixes with yours. While in high school you should find someone that's producing and making beats and book a recording session with them. If that doesn't work, find a hot up-and-coming producer in your area and link up with them. The main goal is to get in the studio so you can create magic.

Fan base: Build your fan base through social media, friendships, live performances, family, participating in high school and community events all while keeping your name and image in the spotlight. You should identify with your fans and pay close attention to what they respond to then feed that hunger.

Promotion: Once you have a finished product to promote you should take advantage of every opportunity to perform or play your music. Make sure you list it on iTunes and all the digital media avenues that are out there for you. Please take the time to research the available markets that will spin your music. Internet radio, Blog radio, Satellite radio,

Local radio, Underground radio, Mixtape sites and more are at your finger-tips. If you can afford to, you should also put a video together and list it online to help build your fan base.

Cross Promote: As a recording artist you will be in a position to make music with other artists such as yourself. By featuring on each other's music you will promote your style to a different market which will in-turn help grow your fan base. If you know of a DJ who's putting out a mixtape, try to get your music featured on it as well. Any chance that you get to work with another artist you should take advantage.

Street Team: Every artist should have a street team that promotes fliers in the streets and on social media. Your team should focus on promotional campaigns on a weekly basis.

Relationships: Relationships play an important part in this profession and can affect your value as an artist. Concert promoters, club DJ's, radio DJ's and party promoters are among the people with whom you should have a relationship. These are the guys who are in touch with your fan base on a daily basis. Remember your main purpose is to get your music played! All of these entities can make this happen, whether in concert, in the club or on the radio.

Cash Flow: Your money will come from unit sales, radio spins, appearances and live performances. To get paid for radio spins make sure that you register your music with Sound Scan, BMI, SESAC and ASCAP. This is where your fan base and promotion pay off. The more people who hear your music the more money you stand to make as an artist. If you create a big enough buzz for your music, the major labels will come calling with money in hand. If you choose to stay independent, you can make cash that way as well. A hit will get you paid! The hotter you are the more you can charge for concerts, performances and appearances.

Talent Agent

Gate Keys

1. Image
2. Character
3. Hard Work and Determination
4. Qualifications and Certifications
5. Good Credit
6. No Criminal Record
7. Clean Driving Record

Estimated Salary: $50,000 - $1,000,000 a year

Certifications: Business License, Tax ID Number, Professional Liability Insurance.

Required age to start: Varies

Behind every great movie, hit TV show, sold-out concert, hot video, commercial, etc. there is a 24-hour, 7 days a week, hustling, talent agent. The agent is responsible for finding work for their client, aka the talent. Talent includes: actors, models, comedians, musicians, recording artists and whatever kind of talent for which there's a market. As a professional talent agent you will need to have a great image, a nose for talent, a strong dedication to the job and most of all, character!

You must be able to sell yourself to your clients as well as the contractors, aka the people that will be contracting your talented clients for their services. This profession will require all of your attention in addition to strong relationships with industry executives. Your lively hood will depend on it, so make sure that you build strong fruitful alliances within the business.

Recruiting Talent: To be a successful agent you will need to have a good eye and ear for talent. Nobody wants to book bad or mediocre talent. So don't just sign anyone to your agency. Apply due diligence and make sure they have the ability to make money first. If you don't see that quality or existing fan base, stay away! Let them go about their business; they will only waste your time and money.

Your roster of talent will represent you and will also attract more talent and potential clients of the same caliber. So be very precise in selecting your business partners. I would research any potential client before doing business with them.

High School is the perfect place to start building relationships with talent and potential clients. The bonds that you can build will be priceless.

Sell Yourself: Everything about you will be on display while in this profession. Things like your clothes, cars, jewelry, cologne, perfume, what you eat, where you eat, your people-skills, etc. Talented people will want to be represented by someone that holds the same qualities as them. Most important is character; good character will take you a long way, even further than money.

Contract agreement: The agreement between you and your talent must be bounded and withstanding while you are representing them. It must state your standard 20% agency fee, the contract duration, any special needs that your talent may desire on their rider, deposit guidelines and more. You can find a general talent agent contract online then adjust it to fit your company.

Clients: Your clients will consist of casting directors, record labels, music producers, magazines, TV and movie studios, promoters, club owners, etc. As an agent you are responsible for booking gigs for your talent, whether it be performing or auditioning they will be counting on you to provide them with streams of income. This is where you will earn your 20% agency fee. So, buckle up and get on your game-face. There's enough money out there for everyone; you just need to go get it!

Rider: A rider is an agreement made between you, your talent and the client. They usually consist of any special requests, like meals, beverages, boarding and travel requests, etc. This can differ between gigs, but it must always be included in the contract before its final.

Deposit: No contract is official without a guaranteed deposit. Before you move forward with any booked gig, get your deposit! Once you receive the deposit you can bind the contract, but be sure to include a clause to receive the balance before the gig is to take place; after you get the rest of your money, the show can go on as planned. Do not proceed with the gig without it! Make no exceptions unless you and your talent agree to it and make sure that it's in writing and signed by all parties, i.e. you, talent and client.

Preferred Markets: The most lucrative markets for talent agents are usually in the major markets. Places like New York, Atlanta, California, Miami, London, Toronto and Chicago can be very lucrative markets. You don't really have to reside in these places to be successful, but you will most definitely need to do business there in order to be successful.

License: You will need a Business license, Tax ID number and professional liability insurance while in this profession.

Cleaning Service

Gate Keys

1. Image
2. Character
3. Hard Work and Determination
4. Qualifications and Certifications
5. Good Credit
6. No Criminal Record
7. Clean Driving Record

Estimated Salary: $50,000 - $1,000,000 a year

Certifications: Business license, Tax ID Number, General Liability Insurance.

Required age to start: 16

Every home, apartment complex, office building and warehouse needs to be cleaned. Most of them have standing contracts with cleaning companies that they count on to: vacuum, sweep, mop, dust, clean bathrooms, wash windows, shampoo carpet and wax floors. As the owner of a cleaning service you'll have tons of money at your fingertips, you'll just need to go get the contracts!

Contracts: You will need to approach businesses to offer your services. If they are interested, you can negotiate prices then. The price shall include an amount that will cover manpower, time, supplies and equipment. Once you both agree on an amount, cleaning schedule and start date then you will be in business!

Experience: The best way to get experience is to get it hands on. While in school, find a cleaning company to work for and get some cleaning experience. This will give you a great feel for the business.

Clients: Empty homes and apartments always need cleaning prior to occupancy. You can contact the property manager, home owner or realtor to put in a bid to clean the dwelling for them.

Office buildings and warehouses occupied and unoccupied will always need cleaning services. Most of the time the office or property manager will be responsible for hiring a service to maintain the cleaning. You will need to visit the office during business hours to discuss putting in a bid to clean their offices. If they already have a contract in place with a cleaning company, still offer to put in a bid when it's time for renewal and always leave a card.

Equipment: In the beginning you will need mops, buckets, vacuums, window cleaning supplies, wax, cleaning chemicals, etc. Once you earn some more income you can purchase some more equipment, like shampooers and buffers. Most business offices already have the basics in their janitor's closet.

License: You will need a business license, Tax ID number and general liability insurance.

GATE KEY

Dancer

Gate Keys

1. Image
2. Character
3. Hard Work and Determination
4. Qualifications and Certifications
5. Good Credit
6. No Criminal Record
7. Clean Driving Record

Estimated Salary: $15,000 - $155,000 a year

Certifications: Love for the Art, Dance Training.

Required age to start: Varies

Professional dancers perform in musicals, plays, videos, commercials, TV shows, movies, community events and also assist with choreography. A great dancer can always find work; it's just beating out the competition for the job that will always stand in your way. So the best chance at guaranteeing a career is to stay at the top of your game at all times while building solid industry relationships. The field is competitive and can take its toll on you, so make sure that this is something you want to do. Staying in shape and being healthy are paramount.

Dancing is a talent that can also be taught; the earlier you start training the better you will be. Usually before accepting a dance gig you will be given the routine to practice before attending the audition or casting. Take every opportunity that you get to dance and make it count; each shot taken will make you better.

Sectors: Dancers have the option to perform in plays, videos, concerts, movies, commercials, TV shows, community events, musicals, etc.

Markets: The best places to work as a dancer are: NYC, Chicago, Hollywood, Atlanta, Las Vegas, Miami and London. Work can be found in any city or town, but the places listed offer the most consistency.

Agent: No matter where you live, you will need an agent to help you find work. A good agent will keep you abreast of current castings and auditions. Depending on their industry relationships they can book you on paid gigs without doing an audition or casting. This however will depend heavily on your skill set as well. So do your research before signing with an agent, make sure that they can deliver for you.

GATE KEY

Sports Management Agency

Gate Keys

1. Image
2. Character
3. Hard Work and Determination
4. Qualifications and Certifications
5. Good Credit
6. No Criminal Record
7. Clean Driving Record

Estimated Salary: $50,000 - $1,000,000 a year

Certifications: Business license, Tax ID Number, Professional Liability Insurance, Background check, Sports Management Training Course (online).

Required age to start: 18

   Sports agents live an exciting fast-paced lifestyle and earn tons of money while representing athletes. A college degree is not required to be a sports agent or run your own sports agency. You are required to register with the athletic organizations as an agent and also with your state. Every state has a different process, so please do your research when applying. The most important key to remember here is that the athlete will be your product and the better they are, the more leverage you will have when dealing with the athletic organizations--this includes NCAA, amateur and the pros.

While in High School you will be in the opportune position to launch your own agency, especially if you have talented athletes in your school. The opportunities will be amazing! Gate Keys 1-6 will need to be implemented at a high level to pull this off. You will be dealing with the big leagues and there is no room for error! I know you're probably in shock right now, but take a moment, re-group, focus and concentrate on getting this money! All the steps you need to make this happen are listed below. Good Luck!

Duties: You will be responsible for contract mediation between athletes and various sports entities as well as potential endorsers. In addition to that you will be expected to give good career advice, negotiate income amounts and manage media awareness. Agents should champion great people skills while promoting their clients. Most importantly you will be responsible for receiving all fees and salaries earned.

Intern: If there's a sports management agency in your area you should apply for an intern position while you're in high school to get your feet wet. If there is not an opportunity for you to intern, you can always take an online course in sports management to give you a perspective.

Athlete: Your talent is your leverage! The better the athlete the more power you will have to negotiate. When recruiting athletes, go for the best! Once you sign them, it will be your job to manage their careers while negotiating the best deals. You may run into some BS from your competition because you don't have the fancy degree, but you have the best athlete, baby! Get paid! You will also have a big advantage if you attend the same high school as the athlete. Keep in mind that you can negotiate with colleges, amateur leagues and the pros.

State Requirements: Every state varies when it comes to registering your sports agency with them to do business. You should contact the County Clerk's Office to inquire about the license you will need to do business as a sports agency and what fees that you'll need to pay. You will also be asked to agree to a background check. *(Make sure you start a Corporation for your business!)*

Registration: You will need to register and get certified with the organization that you plan to do business with, i.e. NBA, NFL, WNBA, NCAA, CBA, CFL, MLB, NHL and Amateur to name a few. Contact their registration offices to get all of the details.

Rates: Agents can choose to get paid the standard 4% - 10% per contract, charge by the hour or charge a flat fee. The decision will be yours to make, every situation will be different.

Knowledge: Before you move forward you should have an in-depth knowledge of the sport that you choose to represent. You should know every athlete and everything about them along with what teams need them and which ones don't. This profession

ANTWAN BANK$

pays well but it won't be easy. If you're going to play with the big boys, you will need to put in the work!

GATE KEY

Business Entities

Corporations, LLC's, LP's

To run a successful business you will need to protect yourself and assets. Selecting the right entity will limit your liability. Each entity has its own benefits; I have listed a few of them below. Anyone of them can be formed for a fee which will depend on your state. These corporations are used by the rich and informed to protect their business and personal financial affairs. (*i.e. Forming an entity is like creating another person to do business for you. This person will take on any fault or liability that may occur while doing business protecting you from harm while also protecting your assets. In the event that someone tries to sue you, they would only be able to sue the business and not you personally.*)

A Business entity can be formed through an Attorney, Online Corporation Services, Secretary of State Department, etc.

Listed below you will find some general information about each entity.

1. **Corporation** (*C and S*): The Corporation is responsible for the activities of the business. In this way the owners or shareholders are protected. The owner's liability is limited to the monies he/she used to start up the corporation, not all of their other personal assets. If an entity is to be sued, it is the corporation that will be sued not the individuals behind the legal entity.

A corporation is owned by its shareholders and managed by its Chairman of the Board, Chief Executive Officer or President. Articles of Incorporation will need to be filed with the state when forming the corporation. Every corporation will need to implement bylaws which will act as their operational road map. The shareholders will not be held personally liable for business debts. Its officers and directors can legally obligate the business. The board of directors will be responsible for management decisions. The C Corporation can be started with one shareholder in most states. The S corporation can have no more than 75 shareholders--no foreign entities, individuals or domestic entities are allowed. Unlike the C corp., the S corporation will need to file form 2533 with the IRS in addition to its bylaws and annual meetings.

The one bad thing about using a C corporation is that its earnings can be taxed twice. This generally happens at the end of the fiscal year (A year from the date the corporation was formed). If the corporation earns a profit, it pays a tax on the gain. If it then decides to pay dividends to its shareholders, the shareholders are taxed again. To avoid the double tax of a C corporation, most C corp. owners make sure there are no profits at the end of the year. This can be done by using allowable write-offs to reduce the net income.

The S corporation however has what we call flow-through taxation which will be explained more in depth later. The S corp. is a flow-through corporate entity. You can file IRS form 2553--"Election by A Small Business Corporation" and the corp. will not be treated as a distinct entity for tax purposes. This will allow profits and losses to flow through to the shareholders as in a partnership.

Note: In the event of death or departure of owner the corporation will continue.

2. **Limited Liability Companies** *(LLC)*: An LLC is good to use in special situations. It will provide the limited liability protection of a corporation and the flow-through taxation of a partnership. The LLC is owned by its members and run by its managers. Articles of organization will need to be filed with the state and a standard operating agreement will need to be in place while in business.

The members will not be held personally liable for business debts. Whether member-managed or managed via upper-management an LLC legally obligates the business and either personnel can make management decisions. An LLC can be started by one member in most states.

Note: In the event of death or departure of owner the

company will be dissolved unless members vote to continue.

3. **Limited Partnership** *(LP's)*: The LP is similar to a general partnership the one difference is that it has two types of partners. The first type is the general partner who is responsible for managing the partnership. This partner has broad powers to obligate the partnership and is also personally liable for the business's debts and claims. If there happens to be more than one general partner involved, they are each liable, meaning that a creditor can go after just one of them for the entire debt.

   The LP is owned by general and limited partners. Its senior manager is the general partner or partners. A certificate of limited partnership will need to be filed with the state and there should be a limited partnership agreement in place while in business. The general partners will be personally liable for business debt; this excludes the limited partners. Only a general partner can legally obligate the business and be responsible for making management decisions. At least one general partner and at least one limited partner are required to start an LP.

   Note: In the event of death or departure of owner the partnership will be automatically dissolved unless provided for in partnership agreement.

GATE KEY

Flow-Through Taxation

LLC - One of the most important benefits of the *LLC* is that the IRS recognizes it as a flow-through tax entity. All of the profit and losses of the business flow through the LLC without tax. They flow through to the business owner's tax return and are dealt with at the individual level.

C Corporation – The C corp. does not offer this feature. In a C corp. the profits are taxed at the corporate level and then taxed again when a dividend is paid to the shareholder. (Thus, the issue of double taxation.) Even still with proper planning, this double taxation can be minimized.

S Corporation – in the S corporation profits and losses flow through, thereby avoiding double taxation, but may only be allocated to the shareholders according to their percentage ownership interest.

Note: You should remember that in an LLC, as with a corporation, you may become personally liable for certain debts of the company, if you sign a personal guarantee.

Note: When operating as an LLC, LP or Corporation the world must be put on notice that you are operating as an independent entity. So always include the appropriate entity after your business name, i.e. Northwest Construction, LLC or Northwest Construction, Incorporated.

Entities to stay away from

Don't let anyone encourage you to go into business as one of the following. The disadvantages far outweigh the advantages.

Sole Proprietorships: In this type of business you will take on all liability personally. It is also hard to sell a sole proprietorship, since its value is based on the owner and not the business. In the event of death the sole proprietorship will terminate. Its successors can only sell assets, not the business as a going concern.

General Partnership: As in the sole proprietorship you will also take on all the risk as a general partnership, but with double the exposure. The partnership will terminate when one partner dies, leaves or goes bankrupt. Most buyers do not want the risk of being in a general partnership which makes it hard to sell your interest.

Licensing

Business License – You will need to acquire a business license in your field of business to operate in your county, city or state. This can usually be obtained at the County Clerk's Office; if not, then they will be able to at least assist you with the process. There is also a fee that will need to be paid when submitting your business license application.

Resale License – This license can also be obtained by going through the same channels that were previously stated. A resale license will be needed, if you plan to sell any goods for a profit while in business.

Tax ID Number or EIN - This can be obtained by calling the IRS--free of charge. Your ID or EIN number will be used when filing taxes. It's the same no matter what type of business or entity you are operating, whether you have no employees or five. You must pay your taxes and I suggest that you get a (CPA) Certified Professional Accountant to file them for you. Trust me! This is a headache waiting to happen, if you don't do it the right way.

Skill Sets

Becoming successful without a degree is not an impossible task. Many have done it before you and many will in the future. You must have the drive, will and dedication to succeed, if this is the path you choose to venture down. There will be sleepless nights along with negativity from your friends and family. But, you must rise above it all and keep your eyes on the prize. Think about why you're doing it and what you want to accomplish. Take that bad energy from the haters and turn it into your motivation to succeed. If you ever feel any doubt about what you are doing, just take a minute and read through the long list of predecessors in the *Fraternity of Successful Dreamers Chapter* that made it, then keep pushing forward. Dreams are what the world is made of, so take your place in it, make your mark and never, ever give up!

Internship: This is where you will have the opportunity to work in your desired profession. The hands on experience that you'll get will be more than worth it and you should cherish every moment. There is usually no compensation while interning; your pay will be the knowledge you gain along the way. If you choose to intern, make certain that you investigate the company and its history. You should select your place of internship based on what you want your future to look like.

High School Educational Skills: Once you've chosen your desired profession, you should build your class schedule to suit it. Enroll in any classes that will help you gain more knowledge in your field. Remember after high school comes the real world, so right here and right now is where you will need to get a head start. Selecting the right courses along with hands-on work will hone your professional skills preparing you for life after high school. Take this very seriously because if you don't put in the work, you will fail!

Here's my perspective. I look at America as a business. With that being said you can choose to be the product, consumer or business partner. Think about that for a second then look at America from each perspective. I've provided you with all the tools to get your journey started while in high school, middle school or even elementary.

Now you can choose to go through life as just a consumer, a product or Business Partner. Giving is the key to success. Take this new found knowledge and become a better person, empower your friends and family as well, then keep thriving to be great! You can do it!

The 7 Gate Keys

Image: First impressions are everything! The way that you dress, speak, smell and how you are groomed speaks volumes to people. Your image should reflect the type of person you are or whom you aspire to be. Present yourself according to your chosen profession and always speak in a professional manor. This is necessary if you want to be taken seriously. Remember you can never get another first impression, so stay ready. Make it a habit!

Character: Your character builds your reputation. Integrity, honesty and courage will stand tall in any situation and are highly measured when it comes to business. It is essential that you be of good character if you want to succeed.

Hard Work and Dedication: These two keys speak for themselves. If you do not have the desire to put in the hard work and dedicate yourself to your chosen profession, then you will get a subpar result. That saying about, "You get out of it what you put in...." is true! Becoming a success with only a High School education will require putting 150% of your time in both hard work and dedication. This is the *action attribute* of the *7 Gate Keys*; it holds all of it together. If you don't put in the work, it will fall apart.

Qualifications and Certifications: Each profession requires some kind of skill set. Some can be obtained in high school, others by interning, taking online courses, skilled training, etc. While yours might be a natural talent, it all comes down to being skilled at a profession. I have done the research for you and listed what is required to become a professional in any career choice listed in this book. When deciding your career path please do not omit the necessary required steps.

Good Credit: Some professions will require a background check where they will look at your credit. Although many of you may not have established any credit yet, you may be surprised at what you'll find in your background check. Parents use kids' social security numbers all the time to get credit cards, cars and put bills in their kids' names. Not to mention the huge identity theft problem we have had since the emergence of the Internet and online hackers.

The main thing to remember here is that credit will establish as soon as you get the first bill in your name. It can be a cell phone bill, light bill, gym membership, it doesn't matter. So pay your bills on time, monitor your credit and make good choices when it comes to sharing your personal information. A bad credit score can ruin your chances at getting a car, bank loan, job, house, apartment, cell phone and more. Now is the time to start monitoring your credit score and building a good credit profile. It will follow you for the rest of your life.

No Criminal Record: So here's something that you probably didn't know as a teen. Once you are considered a felon that moniker will follow you for the rest of your life. It never drops off of your criminal record unless you made a deal early on with the district attorney. The justice system is very flawed and doesn't care who falls victim to it. A misdemeanor doesn't carry as much weight as a felony, but it still follows you forever. If you committed a crime when you were 18, you still will be judged for that same crime 20 years later by employers, business partners, banks, creditors, schools, etc.

Yeah, it sucks, but it's also one of those things about which you need to remain informed. So make sound decisions and don't get caught up in this justice system. We all make mistakes, but the way the system is built, if you are a felon--no matter the crime, whether it be murder, bank robbery, manslaughter, embezzlement, DUI, drugs, theft, etc., it will follow you forever! *(The severity of the crime doesn't matter and rehabilitation won't remove a felony from your record.)*

Tarnishing your record will put you in what I call 'The Trap'! Meaning no matter how hard you try to change, how hard you try to find a decent job, how hard you try to be a productive citizen, you're still a felon with fewer options for success. Society is not built to allow your success, so keep your nose clean and don't get trapped. If this happens to be you — Yes, you!--you still can make it, but you will have to put in 10 times the hard work and dedication, and here, more than ever, your character and image will come into play!

GATE KEY

Fact: America holds the highest amount of people incarcerated in the world. It also is in business with the CCA (Correctional Corporations of America). The CCA is a collective of Private Prisons in the United States. In order to keep their contract with America they have to maintain a quota--keep a certain number of bodies in prison. These prisons get paid a certain amount each year for every prisoner that they house. **Don't be one of them!**

Again, I ask you, what role do you want to play? **Consumer, Product or Business Partner!**

Clean Driving Record: Some of the professions that I've listed require a clean driving record. You should especially take notice of your driving habits, if you fall into these categories. Driving is a privilege and it will be taken away by the state, if violated. Practice good driving habits, like wearing your seat belt, not speeding, not texting or using your cell phone while driving, not driving under the influence, paying attention to pedestrians and road signs, etc.

Facts

Students living in poverty are less likely to attend college than other students. Several other factors can affect college attendance. *-Classroom.synonym.com*

7 in 10 seniors graduate with student loan debt. They then graduate into a bad job market leaving many graduates with little or no job options. *-Projectionstudentdebt.org*

High school graduates without college degrees faced an unemployment rate of 17.9% in 2012 compared to 7.7% for young college graduates. *-Fox17online.com*

Average loan debt $28,400 per student and it is increasing by 6% a year. *-FinAid.org*

Gate Key Challenge

My challenge to you is to network with other student entrepreneurs in your school and build a collective of businesses together where you all can prosper. Contact me via Printhousebooks.com and let me know how it goes. I can't wait to hear about it!

GATE KEY

Parent's Role

Parents I encourage you to help your child with this process. Your insight and support can go a long way on his/her path to success. If you're lucky enough to find yourself in a situation where your kid is not in high school yet or is just entering, take this opportunity to structure his/her high school courses to fit the chosen career path.

There is no better time than now to start building success. Your child can count on you for support while not having to worry about any bills or life's problems right now. They can use this time to build and become successful. Imagine what we could have done, if we had this opportunity in high school. Being informed can make all the difference in the world. If you truly believe in your child and his/her dreams, I beg of you to empower them to succeed.

Thank you for reading Gate Key. I truly hope that it will make a difference in your life. Don't hesitate to leave a review on my Amazon or Barnes & Noble comment forums. I would love to hear from you! If you want to contact me directly, you may do so via Printhousebooks.com

GATE KEY

Other titles available from this Bestselling Author:

MADE: Crime Thriller Trilogy

Adoration

The Party Life

F.I.T.H

Suite 206

The Cover Girl Series *(Three books to date)*

Tahiry

Everlasting Romance

All titles available everywhere books are sold.

www.PrintHousebooks.com

ANTWAN BANK$

PRINTHOUSEBOOKS.com
Read it! Enjoy it! Tell A Friend!
Atlanta, GA.

www.ingramcontent.com/pod-product-compliance
Lightning Source LLC
Chambersburg PA
CBHW032149080426
42735CB00008B/644